GOLF®
MAGAZINE

500
BEST TIPS EVER!

SIMPLE TECHNIQUES TO HELP
YOU IMPROVE YOUR GAME AND
SHOOT LOWER SCORES

GOLF
MAGAZINE
TOP 100 TEACHERS IN AMERICA

with the Top 100 Teachers in America

Edited by David DeNunzio

Time
HOME ENTERTAINMENT

© 2011 Time Home Entertainment Inc.

Published by
Time Home Entertainment Inc.
135 West 50th Street
New York, New York 10020

Some of the material in this book was
previously published in *Golf Magazine*,
and is reprinted with permission by
Time Inc.

ISBN 10: 1-60320-183-1
ISBN 13: 978-1-60320-183-4
Library of Congress Control Number:
2010941132

Printed in U.S.A.

We welcome your comments and
suggestions about
Time Home Entertainment Inc. Books.
Please write to us at:
Time Home Entertainment Inc. Books
Attention: Book Editors
PO Box 11016
Des Moines, IA 50336-1016

If you would like to order any of our
hardcover Collector's Edition books,
please call us at
1-800-327-6388. (Monday through Friday,
7:00 a.m.- 8:00 p.m.; Saturday, 7:00 a.m.-
6:00 p.m. Central Time).

Cover/book design: Paul Ewen

CONTENTS
The best instruction from the best instructors in the game

Your path to lower scores starts here.

GOLF Magazine has published instruction for over a half-century, but never before has it compiled the sheer volume of swing information in a single text as what you'll find in the pages of this book. Whether you're looking to drive the ball farther, putt with greater consistency or expand your shotmaking arsenal, you'll find all the lessons you need right here. In fact, it's safe to say that if the lessons you're looking for aren't part of the 500 presented in this book, than they probably don't exist. Our goal was to provide you with everything you need to know to change your game quickly and shoot lower scores beginning with your next round. With the help of the Top 100 Teachers in America you'll discover that we've done just that.

Unlike the majority of golf instruction manuals, this one focuses primarily on tips—quick-hitting lessons that are easy to understand and, when applied correctly, can make a serious change for the good in your full swing, putting stroke and short game in an instant. You won't have to read and sort through paragraphs of explanation and detail—just look for the area of your game that needs work and apply the fix. These lessons have been proven to get the job done with just a few practice swings or strokes. The secret is to target the weak parts of your game first before making wholesale changes to every facet of your technique. Tip by tip—all 500 of them—you'll see a positive effect on your motion and scores, and that's when the game starts to get fun.

DAVID DENUNZIO
INSTRUCTION EDITOR, GOLF MAGAZINE

SWING BASICS

There's more than one way to maneuver your clubs and get good results. Where you can't improvise is your setup. Here are 37 key start positions to help you make your best swings over and over.

HOW TO BUILD A PICTURE-PERFECT ADDRESS

A six-point stance sets the foundation for success

By Shawn Humphries

The majority of swing errors are the result of mistakes in your setup. Copy the positions here—demonstrated by PGA Tour player Dustin Johnson—to put your backswing on autopilot and set the stage for all the other components of your swing to fall perfectly into place.

1 ALIGN YOUR JOINTS

Check that the balls of your feet, your knees and your shoulders all line up. If they don't, make sure you're not bending too far forward or standing too straight-legged.

2 CHECK YOUR LIE

Regardless of the club you're swinging, the shaft should point at your belt buckle when it's soled properly on the ground.

3 HANG DOWN

The top half of your arms, from your shoulders to your elbows, should from a near-vertical line.

4 DON'T BEND YOUR BACK

Keep your spine straight—a line should connect the back of your shoulders and the back of your head.

5 CLIMB THE LADDER

With good posture, your knees, hips and shoulders are spaced equally apart, like the rungs on a ladder.

6 UNLOCK YOUR KNEES

Bend them slightly and tilt more from your hips. You should feel balanced and ready to move in any direction.

AVOID BAD SHOTS FROM THE START
Stop slices, hooks and everything bad in between with the correct ball position

DRIVER
Even with the outside of your left shoulder

HYBRIDS & FAIRWAY WOODS
Even with your left armpit

PUTTER
Even with your nose

7-IRON THROUGH PITCHING WEDGE
Even with your left cheek

3-IRON THROUGH 6-IRON
Even with your left ear

7

WHERE TO PLAY THE BALL IN YOUR STANCE
My fail-safe guide is easy to learn and recall on the course
By Michael Breed

Rule No. 1 for ball position: The ball should never be left of your left shoulder or right of your nose, regardless of which club you're using. Within this small area, there's an easy way to remember exactly where to position the ball for every shot by using different parts of your body as guides *[see instructions, left]*.

Once you have your ball position set for the particular club in your hand, focus on two things: weight distribution and shaft position. For standard full swings with every club, spread out your weight evenly over both feet, and press the shaft slightly forward by moving your hands toward your target. This combination gives you the best chance to create ball-first contact and solid strikes.

HOW TO SET UP WITH PERFECT POSTURE
Getting this right gives you the on-plane swing you need to hit solid, accurate shots

8
HINGE, BEND AND UNLOCK
Follow this sequence to nail your address
By Scott Sackett

The body angles (spine tilt, knee flex, etc.) that you create at address determine what you can and can't do in your swing. Bad address angles leave you with the type of inconsistent contact that's been ruining your scores. When you create good angles at address, however, you're in better position to make a good swing. Follow the steps at right.

1. Step to the ball with your feet together and the club in the air as shown. Spread your feet to shoulder width while keeping the ball in the right spot in your stance.

2. Lock your knees and bend from your hips. You're looking for about 30 degrees of forward bend, which occurs when your chin is just in front of your toes.

9
FIND THE RIGHT STANCE WIDTH
This easy balance check tells you how far to spread your feet
By Dr. David F. Wright

3. Without disturbing your forward tilt or unlocking your knees, drop your arms down and set your club on the ground.

4. Bend your knees slightly. Don't relax too much—keep your leg muscles engaged. Lastly, tilt your upper body to the right so that your head is behind the ball.

When you're out of balance, one hand will rotate toward your body more than the other. To make sure this doesn't happen, stand straight up in front of a full-length mirror with your feet together. Note how your hands hang at your sides. Next, spread your feet three inches apart, and note your hand position again. Keep changing widths and note the ones that allow your hands and arms to hang exactly the same. At the very least, find three of these perfectly balanced stance widths: one for your wedges, for your mid-irons and for your driver.

10

ANOTHER WAY TO GET PERFECT POSTURE
The club in your hands is all you need
By Brad Brewer

STEP 1
Stand straight up and down and place a club behind the base of your rear end. Make sure your arms and spine are straight.

STEP 2
Tilt from your waist until you feel your weight move onto the balls of your feet.

STEP 3
Swing the club around and sole it on the ground with your arms hanging straight down. Now you're perfect.

11

HOW TO GET AN EVEN WEIGHT DISTRIBUTION
Rock back and forth to find the balance you're missing
By Mitchell Spearman

Stand with your arms at your sides and your feet 18 inches apart. Place your hands on your hips and push your rear end out while tilting your spine forward. Now follow the steps at right.

STEP 1
Rock your weight back until your toes lift off the ground, being careful to maintain your posture.

STEP 2
Rock in the opposite direction, until both heels lift off the ground and all of your weight is in your toes.

STEP 3
Rock back to your normal address posture. You should feel balanced and ready for action.

FIX EVERY FLAW WITH YOUR SETUP
Copy these positions to keep every bad ball flight at bay

Common address mistakes lead to poor shotmaking in bunches. Here's how to correct bad habits at address and elevate your chances of success on each and every swing.

Address Position Checklist
To turn a bad stance into a solid foundation that gives you power and control on every swing, copy the positions in the large photos and avoid the positions shown in the small ones.

By Tim Mahoney

12 ARM HANG
Your arms should dangle freely from your shoulders with the club at its natural lie angle.

CORRECT

TOO STEEP
You're standing too close to the ball.

TOO FLAT
You're standing too far away from the ball.

13 WRIST HINGE
Cock your wrists just enough to set the club at its natural lie with your hands over your toes.

CORRECT

TOO LITTLE
Shaft forms a straight line with your forearms.

TOO MUCH
Creates a steep, outside-in, slice-causing attack.

14 ARM EXTENSION
Hands about two fist-widths from your thighs with driver, and a single fist-width for your irons.

CORRECT

TOO MUCH
Forces you to stand too tall and swing too flat.

TOO LITTLE
Negates swing arc and robs you of speed.

Make it a habit to check your address at least once a month—bad habits are sometimes hard to break.

15

SHOULDER PLANE

Right shoulder slightly lower than the left, about the same distance that your right hand sits below the left on the grip.

CORRECT

TOO LEVEL
Encourages a reverse weight shift.

OPPOSITE
Almost no chance for success from here.

16

HAND POSITION

Hands even with clubface. Don't unduly lean the shaft toward or away from the target.

CORRECT

TOO FAR BACK
Hello, fat and thin contact.

TOO FORWARD
Pulls left shoulder back, inducing a cut.

17

GRIP STRENGTH

Matched to swing speed (see tip No. 24) with unified hands (tip No. 20).

CORRECT

OVER-ROTATED
Moves bottom of swing arc too far forward.

UNDER-ROTATED
Risks poor contact and not squaring the face.

HOW TO TAKE A SOLID HOLD
Your grip is the only connection you have to your clubs, so make sure it's a good one

18

THE NEW WAY TO TAKE YOUR GRIP
This step-by-step plan gives you a perfect hold in 6 seconds flat
By Eric Alpenfels

Learning the right way to hold your clubs (most of you are doing it wrong) will improve your distance and accuracy without you having to make a single change to your swing. Here's how a 6-second grip check can revolutionize your game overnight.

"A 6-second grip check can revolutionize your game overnight."

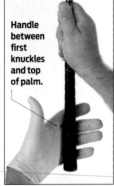

Handle between first knuckles and top of palm.

STEP 1
Hold the club in front of you with your right hand as shown. Set the grip between your first knuckles and the top of the palm on your left hand.

STEP 2
Curl your left-hand pinkie, ring and middle fingers around the handle. Every part of the undersides of these digits should contact the grip.

"Roll" your thumb over.

STEP 3
"Roll" your left thumb over while curling your left index finger around the grip. Press the base of your thumb directly down on the handle.

STEP 4
Slide your right hand toward your left and, just as you did with your left hand, set the grip between your first knuckles and your palm.

STEP 5
Wrap your right pinkie into the fold between your left middle and index fingers, and your right ring and middle fingers around the handle.

"Roll" your thumb over.

STEP 6
Place the lifeline on your right palm over your left thumb by "rolling" your right thumb while curling your right index finger around the handle.

19

HOW TO GET THE RIGHT GRIP PRESSURE

The secret to securing your hold is applying force where you need it the most

By Jon Tattersall

The secret to nailing your grip pressure is to squeeze the handle as hard as you can without affecting your wrist movement. Think "firm hands, soft wrists," which will enable you to control the face yet release the club fully. Try that, along with these other grip-pressure recommendations.

PRESSURE POINT NO. 4
In a good grip your right palm faces the side of the grip. Apply pressure in this direction to activate your wrist hinge.

PRESSURE POINT NO. 1
Pinch the handle tightly into the crease at the top of your palm with your left ring and middle fingers.

PRESSURE POINT NO. 2
With downward pressure, the lifeline on your right palm should fit snugly over your left thumb. If there's space between them, you'll suffer.

PRESSURE POINT NO. 3
Whether you use an overlapping or an interlocking grip, make sure that your right pinkie is applying ample pressure.

PRESSURE POINT NO. 5
If you see any voids between the thumb and forefinger on either hand, pinch those digits together. Pressure here is a must.

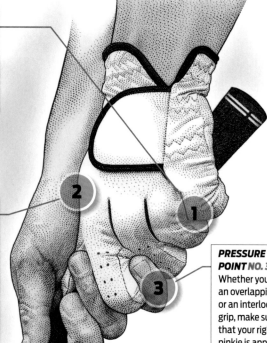

SIX TOP 100 TEACHERS ON:
MAKING YOUR GRIP YOUR OWN
Put these final custom touches on your grip to maximize your control of the clubhead

20
Jason Carbone says
MATCH STRENGTH IN BOTH HANDS

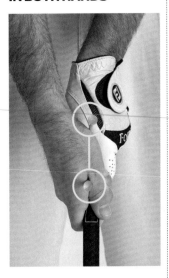

Insert two tees in the creases formed at the base of your thumbs as shown. **Your grip is bad if** one tee points to the right of your grip and the other points to the left. This mismatch of strong and weak holds creates opposing forces in your hands and limits their ability to square the face. **Your grip is good if** the tees form a vertical line. When your hands are aligned like this they can work in the same direction as a single unit and deliver the clubhead to the ball with maximum power.

21
Dr. Jim Suttie says
USE YOUR THUMB FOR CUSTOM CONTROL

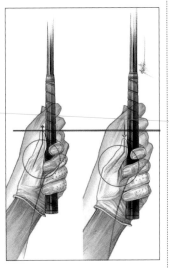

Extend your left thumb if... your predominant poor shot is a hook and/or you lack power. You'll get more of the grip in your left hand instead of your fingers. This prevents the face from closing. **Bend your left thumb** if your predominant poor shot is a slice or you swing past parallel. Flexing your thumb "locks up" your left wrist. This stops your backswing short of full so you can swing down in control and square the face at impact.

22
Dan Pasquariello says
ADOPT A MORE NATURAL HOLD

Stand up straight with your arms resting naturally at your sides. Notice how your left hand hangs. Some players' hands hang with the left palm facing straight back (like mine, pictured here). Other players' handshang with the left palm facing the target, with everyone else somewhere in between. The point is that before you take your grip, **let your left arm hang and then place your left hand on the handle** without changing its position. Make sure you wrap your fingers around the handle, not your palm.

23

Rod Lidenberg says

TAKE A "PALMS-DOWN" APPROACH

Dribble a basketball on the ground, first with one hand and then the other. Notice that to do this you have to turn your palms down toward the ground. Now hold the ball with both arms extended and both palms facing down. Swap the ball for a club and **turn your palms down** as you did before. You should feel that it's significantly easier to get the club in your fingers.

24

Mike Adams says

MATCH GRIP STRENGTH TO HIP SPEED

The faster you turn your hips the more your hands will be ahead of the clubhead as you swing into impact, which has a tendency to open the clubface, which requires a stronger grip. Check your speed by setting up with the leading edge of your 7-iron pressed against the side of a chair. Turn your body into a mock impact position. **If the face rotates open, you need to strengthen your grip** and try it again. Keep strengthening your hold until you can rotate into impact with the face remaining square.

25

Mike Bender says

FLATTEN OUT YOUR KNUCKLES

Take your grip and check your left-hand knuckles. You should see that **the last three fingers of your left hand are quite flat** *[photo, above]*. This indicates that the grip is in the right spot in your hands. If those fingers are sticking out like stairs, you've got the club too much in your palm. Start over until you can get it right every time you take your hold.

HOW TO BUILD A REPEATING SWING
You need a swing you can replicate every time you take your stance over the ball. Here it is.

THE PARALLEL/ PERPENDICULAR SWING
Create an "L" in your backswing and keep repeating it for the consistency your game has been missing

By Shawn Humphries

If you carefully break down the swing into its primary segments you'll find that it's really just a simple repeating pattern of perpendicular and parallel shaft positions. Focusing on these positions and using the segments as checkpoints provides a simple way to replicate your best swing over and over.

26
ADDRESS
Shaft parallel to the ground
When you look down you should see that your right shoulder is lower than your left and that your hands are even with the ball.

27
TAKEAWAY
Shaft parallel to the ground
Your takeaway is a shoulder-dominated move—rock them back like you're trying to hit a 100-foot putt. Once you get the clubhead past your right foot, start hinging your wrists.

28
BACKSWING
Shaft perpendicular to ground
At the end of your takeaway, rotate your forearms and hinge your wrists to create an "L." Move the L to the top by turning your shoulders to create maximum width and power.

31
END YOUR BACKSWING AT ITS NATURAL STOPPING POINT
This drill keeps you from over-swinging and falling off plane
By Ed Ibarguen

Take your normal address position without a club. Slide your right arm underneath your left arm so that the backs of your wrists are touching. Now hook your two first fingers together, matching up the first joint of each finger. Make your usual backswing. You'll notice that the end position of your backswing will be a lot shorter than normal. This is because your left arm can only swing back so far before it begins to bend or you begin to stand up out of your original address.

29
TOP
Shaft parallel to the ground
Lift your arms as you continue to turn—this is what maintains the "L." You've done it right if the angle of your left hand and clubface match up and you've created separation between your right side and your right elbow.

30
FIRST MOVE DOWN
Shaft perpendicular to ground
The key is to let gravity do its thing. Before you start down, make sure your head and shoulders are behind the ball—this gives you the best chance to stay on plane. The transition happens in a flash: your hips "bump" to the left and your arms drop, but your head and shoulders stay back.

HOW TO BUILD A REPEATING SWING
Create an "L" in your backswing and keep repeating it for the consistency you've been missing

"If you've followed the plan to this point, quality impact will happen by itself."

32
DOWNSWING
Shaft parallel to the ground
When your hands reach your right thigh, the club should be parallel to the ground and your target line. Also, the back of the left hand and face of the club match up just like the takeaway.

33
IMPACT
Shaft perpendicular to ground
If you've followed the plan to this point, quality impact will happen by itself. Your impact position should be a mirror of your address position. You'll always make solid contact if your spine and the back of your head are aligned just like they were at address.

34
RELEASE
Shaft parallel to the ground
Your release is an extension of your downswing and impact positions. Keep your right leg passive—this will allow you to rotate the club past your body. Your left leg should form a post. Your arms should swing past it and sling the club through the ball and up to the top.

THE EASY WAY TO MAKE THE MAGIC MOVE
Add lag speed and power by "slotting" the club
By Robert Baker

This drill teaches you to swing your arms down without prematurely releasing (casting) the clubhead. Take any club to the top of your swing with just your right arm. Hold a small plastic bottle against the right side of your torso as shown, then bring your club down to impact. If you can squash the bottle before you unhinge your wrists, you're delaying your release until the moment when it creates the perfect blend of power and accuracy. If you can't, you're casting, and that's bad news for your swing.

35

FOLLOW-THROUGH
Shaft perpendicular
Maintain your spine angle through impact and beyond. You know you're doing it right if the shaft becomes a full extension of your hands and arms.

36

FINISH
Shaft parallel to the ground
Weight balanced over your left foot with everything—knees, hips, shoulders and head—facing the target.

DRIVING

There's more to driving than hitting the ball far. You have to hit it straight, too, and create the right kind of ball flight for the conditions you're facing. Here are 68 easy ways to do it all.

THE BEST ADVICE FOR BAD DRIVERS

38

USE RHYTHM TO ADD YARDS

By PGA Tour player Zach Johnson

If you see me on TV you'll notice that I don't swing very hard compared to some of the other guys on Tour. I prefer good tempo and rhythm over speed. The better tempo you have, the more likely you are to stay on plane, which is the only way you can consistently find the fairway.

I practice my rhythm and tempo at the range by trying to hit 200-yard drives with a full swing. It's harder than you might think—it'll take you a few tries to get the right feel. But once you can start carrying your driver 150 to 175 yards in the air with the shot shape you want, you'll notice how smooth and effortless your swing gets. That's good tempo. Now try to hit your regular distance, but with the same rhythm and feel as your slower swings. You'll be pleasantly surprised by the results.

> "The better tempo you have, the more likely you are to stay on plane."

THE PERFECT DRIVER SETUP
Three ways to nail your tee-box address for big-time yards By Tom Stickney

39
PERFECT SPINE TILT
Step into your address position and, without moving your upper body, place the shaft of your driver along the buttons of your shirt *[photo, right]*. If you're tilted correctly, the shaft will point toward your left foot. You're tilted too much if the shaft points beyond your left foot, and tilted too little if it points to the right of your left foot.

40
PERFECT BALL POSITION
Tee the ball under your left shoulder, the likely spot where your clubhead will be ascending after your swing bottoms out. Sounds easy, but some golfers can't do it consistently because they're preoccupied by foot position. Try this: Set up to the ball, dangle your driver from your left armpit *[photo, right]*, and then look down the shaft to see if the ball is in line with the clubhead.

41
PERFECT BALANCE
You should feel like a middle linebacker, reader to pounce in any direction at address. Add some knee flex and try to settle your weight directly over your shoelaces. That's the best place to put your weight as you start your swing. You don't want to feel like you're over your heels or your toes. Use your laces.

HOW TO MAKE A STRONG BACKSWING

The name of the power game is turning behind the ball and creating as much potential energy as possible

COIL INSTEAD OF TURN

Resistance is distance. Get it by planting your right thigh.

By Brian Mogg

Your typical drive usually comes up short of where you want it to land, which means that you're rotating your shoulders and hips too much or not enough. Ideally you want a 90-degree shoulder turn and 45-degree hip turn, but those measurements aren't critical. In fact, there are a lot of powerful hitters who can't achieve this position. So instead of worrying about degrees, simply turn your shoulders and hips as much as you can while pushing down with a flexed right knee. This will create the resistance and coil you need for driving power.

43
SENSE TENSION

Once you reach the top of your backswing, check that your back is facing the target. If you physically can't rotate that far, at least make sure you've built tension between your upper and lower body.

44
KEEP THE COIL

To fully unlock the power you've stored in your backswing, start your downswing from the ground up. Try to keep the coil in your upper body while your legs, followed by your hips, rotate to the left. The longer you can retain the coil you've stored, the more power you'll impart to the ball.

42
KEEP YOUR RIGHT KNEE FLEXED

From address, slowly turn your shoulders, belly button and torso as far to the right as you can. As you make this slow-motion turn, keep your right knee flexed and your right foot firmly planted on the ground. Feel as though you're pushing your right thigh down into the turf. You'll know you're doing it right if you feel tension between your upper body and your legs.

45

POINT YOUR NOSE AT YOUR RIGHT FOOT
It's the simple way to a strong pivot and weight shift
By John Dahl

You've heard that you need to keep your head still during your backswing. The problem with this theory is that if you try to keep your head still, you'll leave your weight over your left leg. Here's a better swing thought: Move your head just enough for your nose to point at your right foot at the top of your backswing. In this position, you'll know you've transferred your weight to your right side and are in the correct spot to deliver a powerful blow to the ball.

46

SHOW THE TARGET YOUR BACK
It's my personal power move
By PGA Tour player Zach Johnson

In practice and in play I always focus on making sure my back is facing the target at the top of my backswing. Doing this is an efficient way to build power in your swing while also keeping your club on plane. The key is to do it while creating a strong foundation in your right leg. Keep your flex and feel your weight transfer into your right thigh and hip as you swing the club back.

47

HOW TO MAX OUT YOUR TURN
This drill tells you if your rotation is solid or soft
By Steve Atherton, GolfTEC

The more you turn your shoulders, the more rotational power you store up in your backswing—pure and simple. Here's a drill to see where you need to get to. Place a club on the ground perpendicular to the target line and against your right foot *[photo, above]*. Hold your driver across your chest and turn. Your goal is to get the shaft across your chest to point behind the shaft on the ground.

SIX TOP 100 TEACHERS ON:

STAYING ON PLANE

When you fall off, your drives have zero chance of reaching their distance and accuracy potential

48

Tim Mahoney says
FLATTEN OUT YOUR BACKSWING

Most amateurs hit their drives too high, which means they come down too steeply into the ball. Draw a picture in your mind's eye of your hands during your backswing. See **your hands swinging back, but staying below or just even with your right shoulder.** Anything higher will likely result in a steep backswing *[dashed line]*. If you can't make a swing with your driver indoors without fearing that you'll hit the ceiling, you're too high and too steep.

49

Ron Gring says
SHORTEN YOUR RIGHT SIDE

The majority of bad drivers swing the club across the ball from outside the target line to the inside. This swing path creates too much slice-inducing left-to-right spin. To change your path for the good, bend your right side back away from the target as you swing down to the ball—feel like you're "shortening" your right side and **getting your right shoulder lower than your left.** This move ensures that the clubhead arrives from inside the target line.

50

Charlie King says
PRACTICE FROM A SIDEHILL

Here's another way to keep you from making a steep, over-the-top downswing (i.e., the one that usually results in a high slice or a pull): Make practice swings on a sidehill lie with an imaginary ball above your feet. **Swinging from this lie combats a steep downswing,** because if you swing over the top your club will slam into the hill. Focus on swinging around your body rather than up and down, and try to brush the grass where the ball would be in your stance.

51

Robert Baker says
FOLD YOUR RIGHT ELBOW

At just about the time your hands reach knee high, your wrists and your right elbow should start to hinge so that, at the top, **your right forearm and right biceps form the right and bottom sides of a box**. This is a great position to examine to see if you're on plane at the top of your swing, but it's more than a simple checkpoint. Unleashing the fold in your right elbow and your wrists on the way back down gives your swing much more power.

52

Bruce Patterson says
MAKE AN ASCENDING STRIKE

To maximize your drives, you need to hit the ball on the upswing, because this increases your launch angle without adding clubhead loft. **You'll also produce less spin while increasing the force with which you hit the ball.** If you're hitting down on the ball, even as little as 5 degrees, you have virtually no chance with a standard driver to achieve the launch angle and spin rate required for max distance, which for a 90 mph swing is 10 degrees of launch and 3,100 rpm of spin.

53

Ed Ibarguen says
CHECK YOUR CONTACT

Put a thin layer of sunscreen on your driver. Check the face after each practice-range hit and make these adjustments.
Toe Impact: You're standing too far away from the ball or playing the ball too far forward. If your ball position feels correct, swing more from the inside-out.
High Impact: Tee the ball between the sweet spot and the crown, not above the crown as many people suggest.
Heel Impact: You're standing to close to the ball or playing it too far back in your stance. Also, try a steeper backswing.

DRILLS:

9 WAYS TO GROOVE YOUR DRIVER SWING
Hit the range with these proven drills to add serious yards to your tee shots

54

SWING CROSS-HANDED
What It Fixes: *Slicing*
By Keith Lyford

I find that most amateurs never learn how to "turn over" the clubhead through impact. Here's how to fix the problem for good.

STEP 1: Assume your normal setup with your driver and then reverse your hands on the grip.

STEP 2: Start making fast and aggressive practice swings—try to make a "whoosh" sound every time. (If you're not producing a "whoosh," then you need to swing faster.) As you swing through impact, feel how the reverse grip makes it easy to turn your top hand over your bottom hand at the bottom of your swing..

STEP 3: Take your normal grip and immediately hit a couple of drives. The proper feeling of fully releasing the clubhead should still be very strong and you should feel your swing speed pick up dramatically through impact.

55

60-SECOND BACKSWING
What It Fixes:
Swing inconsistency
By Mike Malaska

Make your backswing last an entire minute. As you perform this drill the club should literally move at a snail's pace. Don't just swing to the positions and stop—the motion should be extra slow, but you should never stop moving. Keep in mind that this is more of a workout than you might think (you'll see what I mean as soon as you get to the top).

56

"Through impact, use 'butt power' to whip your left hip up and around while keeping your chest still."

—Robert Baker

57

TWO-CLUB SWING CHECK
What It Fixes:
Bad starts
By Dana Rader

Take your regular grip with any iron. Turn a second iron upside down and place it in your hands as shown. Make your regular backswing and stop when your hands reach chest height. If the shaft points between the ball and your feet, your backswing is too steep—add more shoulder turn. If the shaft points to the far side of the ball, your backswing is too flat—add wrist hinge. You want the shaft to point at the ball.

58
PLANT YOUR LEFT SIDE

What It Fixes:w

Reverse weight shift

By PGA Tour player
Hunter Mahan

Try to make a big backswing turn and then start your downswing with your legs and get your weight to your left side. When you're about halfway down, you should feel like you're firing your weight against your left leg. The last thing you want to do is to hang back on your right side and hit a weak slice.

59
THUMB GRIP

What It Fixes:

Too-narrow swing arc

By Brad Brewer

Take a grip with only your thumbs and index fingers on the handle as shown. Start your swing by pushing the left side of the grip back with your left thumb and index finger. Add just a touch of shoulder and hip turn. Feel how the clubhead extends naturally back along your target line with the toe of the club pointing up. This makes your swing arc as wide as it can be, giving you extra power without having to swing harder or faster.

60
SET THE SHAFT AT 45 DEGREES

What it Fixes:

Swinging off plane

By Bruce Patterson

Studies show that your clubshaft should sit at an angle between 45 to 47 degrees as you swing into impact (very

45°

similar to the ideal shaft angle at address). Since it's hard to know for sure what 45 degrees feels like, set up using a square box as a guide. Set the heel of your driver against the far lower corner of the box, then adjust your stance so that the shaft crosses the high near corner. Now you're set.

61

"Start down to the ball by rolling onto the inside of your right foot and the outside of your left foot."

—Paul Marchand

62
DRAW AN "XL"

What it Fixes:

Chicken-winging

By Laird Small

After impact, allow your left elbow to fold and your right forearm to cross over your left. Picture your left arm and shaft forming a capital "L." This will help you properly fold your left elbow. As far as your forearms are concerned, picture them making a capital "X" as your right forearm rolls over your left and squares the clubface.

HOW TO HIT MORE FAIRWAYS
Follow these moves to tighten your dispersion pattern and find the short stuff more often

VISUALIZE THE RIGHT PATH

This range drill shows you where your misses are coming from
By Martin Hall

You can't make contact on the center of the clubface with your driver, and that's costing you distance and accuracy.

DRILL: Change Your Lane

Lay four dowels (or four irons, or even string) on the ground as shown. The spaces between the dowels should be slightly wider than your clubhead. Address an imaginary ball in the middle lane, then follow the checkpoints at right.

Fixes heel hits

Fixes toe hits

63

If you tend to hit it off the toe...
Make sure your clubhead travels through the far lane after impact (swing more inside-out).

64

If you tend to hit it off the heel (or tend to shank your irons)...
Make sure your clubhead travels through the near lane after impact (swing less inside-out).

65

Once you correct these mistakes....
Keep practicing. After 10 practice swings, tee up a ball and swing away. Now that you're slotted correctly, you'll hit it square and the same distance every time.

66

BISECT YOUR BICEPS
This is the position to master for straight hits
By PGA Tour player Rickie Fowler

Good drivers start their downswings with their hips. This lower-body-activated downswing creates separation between the upper and lower body. This is the true source of accuracy in any golf swing because the shaft responds to the separation by dropping down and onto the ideal plane. I know I'm doing it correctly when the shaft bisects my right forearm when my hands reach waist-high in my downswing.

67

SHORTEN YOUR FINISH FOR SAFER DRIVING
Try this quick tip to split the fairway every time
By Martin Hall

Instead of swinging into your normal full follow-through, finish your drives when the clubhead reaches about waist high after impact. Call this spot "Checkpoint Charlie," and go through the following list when you reach it:

● **The clubshaft and your left arm are more or less still in line.**
● **Your right wrist is still bent back.**
● **Your right arm is across your chest.**
● **Your chest is facing the target.**
● **The toe of the club is pointing up.**

If your shortened finish satisfies the five conditions above, you may lose a little distance, but you'll also land a lot more shots on the short grass.

68

HOLD THE CLUB IN THE CORRECT HAND
Getting this right aims you straight every time
By Dr. David Wright

Holding the club in one hand—not two—as you pick your target naturally squares your body to the target line, but first you need to know which hand to use. For most of you, holding the club in your right hand will open your shoulders and holding the club in your left hand will square them. For others, the reverse is true. To find out for sure, stand facing a corner of a room. Pick up the club with your left hand and then with your right hand. The visual aid of the corner will make it obvious which hand you should use.

OPEN   SQUARE

THE DRIVING GRID:

21 ANSWERS TO YOUR DRIVING QUESTIONS

Quick ways to blast it farther, hit it straighter and dominate from the tee box

	Top 100 Teacher **MIKE ADAMS**	*Top 100 Teacher* **MARTIN HALL**	*Top 100 Teacher* **DAVE PHILLIPS**
Q What's the best move to increase driver accuracy?	**69** Set up on your knees and swing. When you can't go back anymore, hold this position. That's your stop point—anything longer and you risk hitting off line. 	**72** Make sure that your grip is firm and your wrists are soft. **Waggle the club back and forth at address.**  You see Tour pros waggle all the time—and there's a method to their madness.	**75** Make your regular full swing with your driver and stop your downswing at belt height. Check your left knee: Is it closer to the target than your left hip? **When your left knee beats your left hip to your left foot, you lose your left-side post** and have nothing to hit against. It's like taking a baseball swing on ice.
Q What's the driving basic I can't do without?	**70** Address an imaginary ball with a towel held under your armpits and draped across your chest. **Make swings with the towel under your arm,** making sure you don't drop the towel. The drill teaches you to fold your arms correctly (right arm folds in your takeaway, left arm folds in your follow-through).	**73** **Place a dollop of shaving cream on the left side of your chin.** Make your regular backswing and then check your left shoulder. If your left shoulder isn't caked with shaving cream, then you rotated your shoulder under your chin. Try the drill again, and this time make an effort to turn your left shoulder into your chin.	**76** Drive your **right knee and right hip as** a single unit. Make slow swings to ingrain the feel. 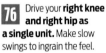 Focus on returning your right knee and hip to impact at the same time.
Q What's the easiest way I can speed up my swing?	**71** **Drop your right foot back** a full foot's length at address. Doing this allows you to make a bigger shoulder turn during your backswing—the secret to adding yards to your drives.	**74** **Make three 1-inch moves:** 1) Move the base of your spine one inch closer to the target; 2) pull your right shoulder back one inch from its usual setup position; and 3) play the ball one inch back of where you usually position it in your stance. These simple adjustments turn your usual address into a launching pad.	**77** Increase the width of your swing by getting **more arm height.** If you don't have ample flexibility in your shoulder joint, find a stretching pole or broom and try the exercise at left to increase your range of motion.

PGA Tour Player	*Top 100 Teacher*	*Top 100 Teacher*	*Top 100 Teacher*
SERGIO GARCIA	**TOM STICKNEY**	**RON GRING**	**CHARLIE KING**

78 Hold your chin up, and keep it there. If you bury it into your chest, you won't have room to swing through impact. **Your right shoulder should work under—not into—your chin on your downswing.**

81 Grab two headcovers and wedge each one into your armpits. Make a few hip-high to hip-high practice swings and try to hold the headcovers in place. You know you're doing it right if you **feel your upper body and arms moving as single unit**—this is how you must rotate your body.

84 **As you take the club back, keep your left arm parallel to the ground.** This helps you extend both arms during your backswing, which is critical to setting them in the right position to create accurate speed in your downswing.

87 Grip your driver with just your left hand. Swing into impact and stop. The trick is to **swing your arm down while also** **rotating it** so that at impact your left elbow points slightly behind you.

---

79 I there's one thing that really pulls it all together for me it's **dropping my hands and arms straight down** from the top of my backswing.

82 Every time you step onto the tee, run through your checklist and make your decisions while standing behind the ball. Then let it all go. As soon as you step over the ball, your focus is where you want it to go. **Never make changes or think of anything else while you're over the ball.** If something comes up, step away.

85 From the top, keep your left arm as straight as possible, but do it while aggressively bending your right elbow. **This is the easy way to add powerful clubhead lag** to your motion.

88 Make practice swings from an uphill lie (back foot lower than the front). Almost automatically, the **uphill lie gives you the upward angle you need to hit powerful drives.** When you move to flatter ground, resist moving forward—use your left side as a post that your club can sling up to and past.

---

80 **The secret is to swing within yourself.** If you swing at 100 miles per hour and hit it on the toe, you won't hit the ball as far as you would with an 80-mph swing that catches the ball in the center of the clubface. My average clubhead speed with a driver is 118 mph. That's fast, but I can—and sometimes do—swing faster.

83 Picture **moving your right shoulder behind your right ear.** Not only does this give you a stronger rotation, it keeps your spine angle intact.

86 "Crack the whip" by extending both arms as you swing through the ball. This "wide" position is what sends your swing speed off the charts. It should **feel like you're transferring the energy stored in your bent right elbow to the ball as you straighten both arms.** The longer they remain straight, the better.

89 Grip the shaft of your driver near the hosel and make a few practice swings. Make sure the  "whoosh" sound is loudest just in front of where the ball would be.

STRATEGY:

THE GO-TO DRIVER SHOT
Try this savvy swing thought when you have trouble finding the fairway

 90

DROP-KICK YOUR DRIVES
Making this common mistake reduces slice and hook spin
By Jon Tattersall

Y ou usually swing your driver on too steep an angle of attack. The result is drives that have both too much spin and too much height. An easy way to stop this error is to drop-kick your driver. You've likely drop-kicked it before (though not on purpose), and the resulting shot probably didn't peel off radically to the left or right. That's because it didn't have much sidespin, a welcome benefit when you ascend into the ball.

HOW TO DO IT
STEP 1 At the driving range, place a tee in the ground and make some practice swings in which the sole of your driver hits the ground before you hit the tee. Try to contact the ground with the sole of your club 6 to 8 inches behind the ball. The club shouldn't dig into the ground, but bounce off the turf and into the tee.
STEP 2 Once you have this feeling, place a ball on the tee and try hitting it with the same drop-kick method. You'll probably notice that the ball flies straighter than normal.
STEP 3 Now hit some drives without hitting the ground first. Try to retain the feel of swinging up on the ball, rather than down. You should see the ball launch higher and fly straighter than normal. And because your angle of attack is flatter, you should gain noticeable distance as well.

Hitting the ground before the ball with your driver is good practice for learning to swing up into the ball.

Hit the turf here.

PLAN A PERFECT TEE BALL
Three musts for getting into Position "A" By PGA Tour player Jim Furyk

Today's equipment is so advanced that you don't need a picture-perfect swing to hit the fairway. But even I struggle off the tee if I don't follow the rules below.

91
EYE TROUBLE
Find the trouble and then throttle back. The trees beyond the fairway here sit 268 yards from the tee. I'll risk reaching them if I hit driver, but I can hit a 3-wood all day long and always be safe. That being said, opt for the safest play unless it puts you at too large of a disadvantage. Hitting a 4-iron off the tee isn't a good idea if it leaves you with a 4-iron into the green.

92
GET WIDE
If you're able, make a "safe driving" book for your course, marking the widest section of each fairway. It could be at 200 yards or 270 yards. I do this all of the time on Tour. My book shows me the safest area when I absolutely have to hit a fairway. If you're not sure where the safest landing area is, look for the 150-yard post—it's usually placed in a decent spot.

93
BUY SOME ACCURACY
You hit your 3-wood better than driver for one simple reason: a 3-wood has more loft. Make the switch to an 11- or 12-degree driver. The extra loft will give you more backspin, and more backspin always means less sidespin. You'll drive it straighter as a result.

SIX TOP 100 TEACHERS ON:

SWINGING FASTER WITH LESS EFFORT
How to ramp up your swing speed without swinging out of your spikes

94	**95**	**96**

Mike Adams says
FAVOR A NARROW STANCE

Brady Riggs says
DON'T FORGET TO SWIVEL YOUR HEAD

Glen Deck says
MAKE A CREASE IN YOUR PANTS

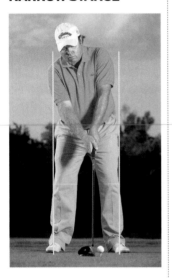

Position your feet directly under your hips. This "stacks" the upper part of each leg on top of the lower, giving you full use of the power of your entire leg. In addition to giving your swing extra leg power, **a hip-width stance makes it easier to pivot around each hip.** This is a fundamental of any striking motion. If your stance is wider than your hips, you'll need to move laterally to get either hip where you need it, and with all that sliding you're bound to reverse pivot and hit a major-league slice.

When you try—as you've probably been told a thousand times—to keep your head still during your full swing, you restrict your ability to make a full turn and your distance potential drops. **Swiveling your head, on the other hand, allows you to make a bigger shoulder turn,** and that's a quick way to hit longer tee shots. The key to this move is to keep it natural. Don't jerk your head to the right in the backswing—just allow it to be carried along by the rest of your turning body.

To create power on your downswing you have to plant your left foot before you step on the gas. That's what teachers call "creating leverage." Look at a photo of any Tour player swinging down from the top and you'll see that they **have a stretch on both sides of their pants above the knees.** These creases indicate that they're posting their left side and creating power from the ground up. You need to learn to create this same look if you want to drive it longer.

97
Robert Baker says
KICK IN YOUR RIGHT KNEE

S tart your downswing by kicking in your right knee toward the target. This gets your weight correctly moving left, and it also moves the bottom of your swing arc forward where it needs to be and **jump-starts your pivot toward the target.** It's as simple as it sounds, but you also need to roll your ankles toward the target and lift your right heel. It should feel like the toes of your right foot are pushing your right knee toward your left.

98
Steve Atherton says
MUSCLE UP TO BUILD HAND STRENGTH

A firm grip pressure helps you control the clubface as you build more speed, but this shouldn't come at the expense of keeping your wrists soft. The trick is to **increase your hand strength until a "loose" grip is as strong as your current "tight" grip.** Try wrist curls at the gym or use a squeeze ball at your desk. You can also search the web for hand-strengthening drills—there's a lot out there.

99
Mike Malaska says
ADD SOME FOREARM ROLL

W ith only your left hand on the club, set your left arm into the downswing delivery position. Then, swing the club into your release. As you do, keep your left arm attached to the left portion of your chest, but **roll your forearm so that the back of your glove points at the target at impact and at your left hip in your release.** The lesson? There's more left arm roll than swing through impact. A great way to think of this is that your left elbow is the hub of the wheel and your left hand is a spoke.

NEW METHODS:

MAKE YOUR BEST MOVE WITH THE O-FACTOR

The O-Factor, a rarely discussed move but clearly evident in the swings of the game's elite players, will make you longer and more accurate with every club, especially your driver. Your hips are the key.
By Robert Baker

There are dozens of ways to increase the speed of your swing and pound the ball farther off the tee, but when you increase the oomph, you put additional emphasis on the need to hit the ball straight— the harder you hit the ball, the farther into the weeds it's going to fly if you don't square the clubface up perfectly at impact. The longest hitters in the history of the game—from Nicklaus to Norman to Woods—understood that the secret to launching massive, straight drives is an aggressive and powerful hip turn that starts immediately as you begin your downswing and pulls your left hip not only to the left of the target, but also up. This raised left hip is your O-Factor, and the greater its angle, the better. It's a simple move that sends your swing speed off the charts and, better yet, works with every club in your bag.

100 **O-FACTOR ADDRESS**
Set your body like an airplane coming in for a landing, with your left shoulder and left hip above their right-side counterparts and your spine tilted away from the target.

O-POSITIVE
At address, your O-Factor should be slightly positive. As you settle into your stance, bump your left hip up to set your body at the correct angle.

101 O-FACTOR BACKSWING

Turn against the resistance of your right thigh, not your entire lower body, and make sure you rotate your shoulders and your hips. This allows you to create maximum energy.

102 O-FACTOR DOWNSWING

From the top, turn your hips immediately to the left and, as the club approaches impact, pull your left hip up. This creates whip-like speed and helps drop your club onto the correct plane.

O-NEUTRAL
You're balanced and loaded up with power if your hip angle shifts back to zero while your spine remains tilted away from the target.

O-POSITIVE
The secret to power is creating a positive O-Factor through impact. Your left hip moves up and your right shoulder stays down.

LEARN FROM THE BEST:

DRIVE IT LIKE DUSTIN JOHNSON

Try my speed and power moves to shorten every hole you play By PGA Tour player Dustin Johnson

I've always hit the ball far, but I continue to pick up yards every season thanks to the work my coach, Allen Terrell, puts into my swing. Getting holes off to good starts with great drives is critical. Think about it—how much could you lower your handicap if you added 20 yards to your tee ball and never missed a fairway?

MINIMIZE YOUR ANGLES
Make a more level turn so you don't get bent and stuck

From the top, think about keeping your knees stable or at the same height as they were at address. This helps you remain tall so you have enough space when you swing through impact. I like to picture a dot on my right hip, and try to keep that dot at the same height while I move it closer to the target during my downswing hip turn. Notice that when I do this *[photos, below]*, my knees remain stable and my belt line stays horizontal to the ground. All good stuff.

STEP 1
Picture a dot on your right hip.

STEP 2
As you turn, keep the dot at the same height and your knees stable.

STEP 3
Do it right and you'll have level hips and ample space to fire your driver through impact.

TAKE AN ATHLETIC STANCE
Set up like an athlete to hit like one

I've spent countless hours perfecting this part of my game—when it's right, I'll contend; when it's off, I'm in danger of missing the cut. The most important thing to build into your address is a feeling of athleticism, like you had when you played basketball and were guarding someone off the dribble, or settling in at shortstop to field anything that came your way. Here's how to get it:

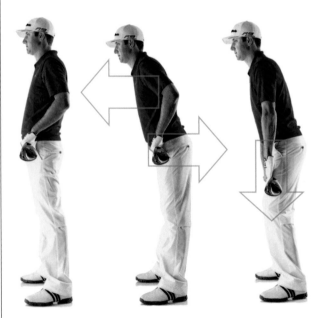

STEP 1
Stand erect and place your driver across your belt line.

STEP 2
Push the shaft into your body. React by leaning your upper body forward and pushing out your rear.

STEP 3
Unlock your knees and push the shaft down your quads. Feel your weight move into your legs and feet.

105

REV UP YOUR SWING SPEED
Increase the distance from your right ear to your hands
Regardless of the club you're swinging, you can easily build extra speed by making your swing arc as wide as it can be. I do this by taking away the club nice and low, which not only widens my swing arc but also stops the common tendency to lift the club up. As you take the clubhead away low, turn your shoulders while keeping your hands as far away from your right ear as possible [photo, above]. Once you're set, swing your right arm down so that you actually increase the distance between your right ear and your hands. Your swing speed will skyrocket.

IRON PLAY

You've hit the fairway—time to get the ball on and close. This requires consistent technique with every iron in your bag. The following 62 tips will have you peppering the pin in no time.

106

NAIL THE MOMENT OF TRUTH

They key to iron consistency is consistent impact

By Mike Davis

Most players try to hit their irons better by swinging harder, but trying to manipulate speed only saps power and accuracy. That's because your arms outrace your body and reach the ball before you're able to shift your weight—your true power source.

The key is to consistently arrive at impact with a slightly descending blow. What does that look like? Check the photo at right. You're doing it right if the shaft of your club is ahead of the clubhead at impact, your weight is over your left foot and your hips feel open to the target. These positions indicate that your arms and hips are moving at the same pace—an absolute must.

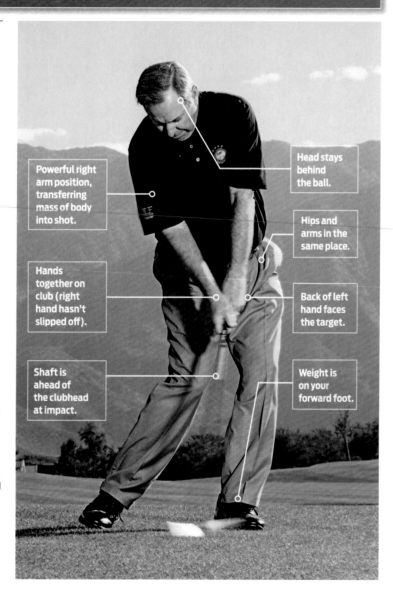

Powerful right arm position, transferring mass of body into shot.

Head stays behind the ball.

Hips and arms in the same place.

Hands together on club (right hand hasn't slipped off).

Back of left hand faces the target.

Shaft is ahead of the clubhead at impact.

Weight is on your forward foot.

THREE WAYS TO NAIL YOUR IRONS

These basic moves cause the quality of your ballstriking to skyrocket

COPY THIS!

By Jon Tattersall

Looking for new ways to turn glancing blows into pure strikes that never leave the pin? Search no further than the following three moves, which combined give you the width to add speed and the turn and shift motions that help you arrive at impact in all the right positions.

107

KEEP YOUR LEFT ARM STRAIGHT

It creates a wide arc and more power

Good golfers keep their left arm straight. They're able to do this because their right shoulder is flexible enough to support the left-arm extension (when your right shoulder can no longer support it, your left arm bends). Stretching will help, as will making a conscious effort to keep your left arm as straight as possible on your backswing and on the way back down. As you swing to the top, fold your right elbow to support this action.

108

PUSH OFF AND UP

Explode into impact with a leaping action

On your backswing, push your weight through your right foot and into the ground. On your downswing, release this loaded energy by pushing *off* the ground, exploding upward—feel like you're leaping off the ground but keeping your spine angle intact. You'll know you're doing it correctly if your left hip is higher at impact than it was at the top of your backswing.

109

LOAD ON EACH LEG

Put your pins to work for extra speed and accuracy

Although you address the ball standing on both legs, each is independently loaded, exploded off of, and stabilized to create power and support during different parts of your motion. When the stability in any leg breaks down, your ability to produce max power instantly goes kaput.

As you move into your downswing, all you have to do is get your weight into your left leg. Avoid falling back at all costs.

FIVE WAYS TO SWING ON PLANE
These tested tricks keep you on the correct path going back and going through

DIAL IN YOUR BACKSWING
Use the image of a clock to set your shaft and clubface in all the right positions
By Michael Breed

Set up like you normally do, but imagine a giant clock on a wall to your immediate right. Make your backswing and hold your top position. Ask a friend to tell you at which time the shaft is pointing.

 110

You're In Danger of Hitting It Fat If...
The shaft crosses anywhere later than 2:00. This tells you that your backswing is much too flat, with the clubface closed.

 111

You're In Danger of Hitting It High and Right If...
The shaft crosses anywhere earlier than 2:00. This tells you that your swing is too steep and your clubface is open.

 112

You're In Position for Solid Contact If...
The shaft crosses 2:00 on the dot. When you reach this position, you're correctly on plane and set to deliver a centered strike.

113

HOW TO KEEP YOUR CLUBFACE SQUARE
Watch your watch to stop rotating the face open or closed
By Peter Krause

While wearing your wristwatch, start your swing and then stop it when your hands reach shoulder height. Look back and see if you can tell the time on your watch *[photo, left]*. If you can't see the face of your watch, you've taken the club up on too steep of a plane. That can lead to a slice. To fix this, swing your club more around your body in an arc, like a satellite in orbit. That doesn't mean whipping the club to the inside with your arms. Rotate your left forearm as you swing your arms up in front of your chest. Now you can attack the ball on an inside-out path—the key to pure shots.

114

RELEASE FOR PURE STRIKES
It's what you do after impact that counts
By Robert Baker

Through the hitting zone, gradually rotate your forearms (right over left) and turn your wrists so that your left-hand knuckles and left elbow point toward the ground in your release. Pointing your knuckles downward works because maximum acceleration occurs when your hands give in to the force of your downswing and turn over to release the clubhead toe over heel. The next time you practice, make an effort to sling the club smoothly past your left thigh by trying to "flick" an imaginary object off your left thumb. Or think of how you'd turn your left hand out to hitch a ride.

GROOVING A SWEET IRON SWING
Try these proven moves and drills to iron out the kinks in your motion

---

115

Kip Puterbaugh says
AVOID DOWNSWING "TROTTER'S" KNEE

NO!

Bring a small wastebasket to the range and hit iron shots with the bin placed just inside your right big toe. If you hit the bucket, your right knee is moving out or to the right of the target, what instructors call "trotter's knee." It's bad news because it completely robs you of leverage. **Your right knee should move toward the target** (or even slightly left of the target). It's an important move that allows you to roll off the inside of your right foot so you can shift your weight and spin your hips.

116

Carl Rabito says
CHECK FOR A REVERSE WEIGHT SHIFT

Take your address position and swing the club to the top with your right arm only. If you correctly move your body and weight behind the ball, **your left arm will hang directly over your right thigh.** If you reverse your weight shift and lift the club up in the air, your left arm will hang over your left thigh. Use this drill as a pre-round warmup or whenever you start to spray it off the tee or fairway.

117

David Glenz says
CREATE A SOLID, DESCENDING STRIKE

Hit balls from an area where some tall grass meets some nicely mown grass. Set up so that the mown grass is on the backswing side of the ball. Hitting from this lie teaches you to properly strike down on the ball and **contact the ground in front of the ball.** If you hit behind the ball like you're doing now, you'll feel your clubhead lag through the grass behind the ball and decelerate quickly. Do it correctly and you'll miss the grass behind the ball and the ball will rocket off your clubface.

118

Dr. Jim Suttie says
SET YOUR ELBOWS LEVEL AT THE TOP

Copy the photo above. You can see how my elbows are level and the club is parallel to the target line. This position promotes a proper swing path that comes just slightly from the inside, which is the most direct and consistent route to the ball. The simple fact is, **if you don't have balanced elbows you're going to have to make compensations** during your downswing that will lead to a lot of inconsistent shots.

119

Brad Redding says
HINGE AND TURN FOR CONSISTENCY

A good backswing requires that you **use your body, arms and hands in equal amounts**—overdoing one or the others tends to maneuver the club off plane. To learn exactly how to do this, hold the club out in front of you and press the heel pad of your left hand against the grip while pulling the shaft toward you with your right index finger *[inset photo]*. This is the action you need in your wrists to hinge the club onto the desired plane. Now simply turn your chest and back away from the target *[large photo]*.

120

Bill Moretti says
STAY IN YOUR ADDRESS POSTURE

Use this trick to see if you're losing your posture when you swing. Tuck a book in the back of your pants so half of it shows above your belt. As you bend forward into your address posture keep the exposed part of the book flat against your back. Now make your regular full swing. If you start to raise up, the book will press into your back. If you drop too far down, you'll lose contact with the cover. Keep making swings (in slow motion, if you have to) until you can **keep the book snug against your spine all the way.**

IRON SWING MUSTS & NEEDS
These basics are the secret to fine-tuning your technique for consistently solid strikes

121
CREATE ROOM FOR A POWER IMPACT
Moving closer to the ball is no good for your game
By Mike Malaska

Moving your hips and midsection closer to the ball through impact is an error that typically leads to weak shots that leak to the right and overall poor ballstriking. Here's how to stop making this mistake:
1) Set up with your backside against your golf bag.
2) Swing while maintaining contact with the bag.
The secret is to focus on each cheek: Touch the bag with your right cheek on your backswing, and with your left cheek on your downswing.

123
NAIL YOUR TOP POSITION
A split grip does the trick
By Bill Forrest

As you make your backswing, slide your right hand to the bottom of the grip *[photo, above]*. Notice how this causes your right elbow to fold and your left arm to stay straight and stretch across your chest instead of lifting up. These are key moves for staying on plane.

122
ADD SOME LAG
This is the true secret to extra power
By Mitchell Spearman

Grab an iron by its hosel and make the widest backswing you can while keeping both arms straight. Now, drop your hands down toward your right pants pocket as fast as you can. Notice how when you perform this drill your swing arc goes from wide to narrow, and how your wrists automatically hinge to their max capacity. In an instant, you look like Sergio Garcia, the modern-day poster child for clubhead lag.

STEP 1　　　**STEP 2**

124
TILT FOR SOLID STRIKES
Standing over the ball leads to poor contact
By Scott Sackett

Take a look at your grip. Notice that your right hand is lower than your left. So unless your right arm is five inches longer than your left (not likely), your right arm, shoulder and right side of your head should be lower than their counterparts. This means that you should be tilted at least a couple of inches to the right at both address and at impact.

125
PICTURE THE PERFECT SWING
You have to know what one looks like before you can make one
By Mike Lopuszynski

Most golfers are taught to swing down the target line. The only time your clubface should point down the target line, however, is when you contact the ball. In this photo, the balls lined up on the tee show where the clubhead should be at every point in your swing. The swing path starts inside and intersects the target line only just before impact and then starts back inside right after impact.

126
FIND YOUR IDEAL SWING PLANE
This personal touch makes your swing easier to repeat
By Peter Kostis

Place the shaft of any club over your left shoulder and lift your left arm so that the underside of your lead forearm rests on the shaft. This is your correct swing plane. If your left arm is higher than this, then your swing is too steep. If your left arm is lower than the checkpoint, then you're too flat.

127
STRETCH OUT YOUR BACKSWING
Tension equals energy
By Todd Sones

As you take the club to the top, feel like you're stretching the butt of your club away from your left foot while keeping your left heel planted on the ground and your weight on your left side. Imagine a rubber band connecting your left foot and left hand. With your left side stretched taught like this at the top of your backswing, you're in the most powerful position possible.

HOW TO PRACTICE YOUR IRON SWING
Make your range time serious learning time with the following drills

HOW TO PERFECT YOUR SWING PATH
Use my quad method and never cut across the ball or push it right again
By Dr. Jim Suttie

Most amateurs don't know how to swing from inside the target line to outside and instead do the opposite. The result is poorly struck shots that leak to the right or slice quite a bit. You have to learn to swing inside-out. To do so, lay two irons on your target line on both sides of a slightly teed ball, and then lay two others on a 45-degree line to your target line. Label each club in your mind as shown.

128 GET YOUR AIM RIGHT
Address the ball and aim down club No. 1. Make sure your clubface is perpendicular to the butt of the club (i.e., aiming straight down the target line).

129 AVOID AN INSIDE TAKEAWAY
Once set, take the club in your hands back along club No. 2. This should feel a bit more outside than what you're used to. Accept the feeling.

131 AVOID THE CUT
As you move through impact and beyond, try to swing over club No. 4. This is a natural extension of your inside downswing approach, and further stops you from cutting across the ball.

130 HIT FROM THE INSIDE
On your downswing, try to swing along club No. 3. This is the correct inside path to the ball that all great ballstrikers travel on.

Follow the numbered clubs in slow motion at first. You should get the feeling of swinging inside out—maybe for the first time ever. Once you groove the feel, go for it at full speed. You'll see improvement almost immediately.

132

SWING MORE AROUND THAN UP AND DOWN
The correct plane is flatter than you think
By Charlie King

Make practice swings as though the ball is on a tee at waist height. Shape your swing around your body and point the butt of the club at the imaginary ball throughout this mock swing. Swing repeatedly back and through. This drill shapes your swing so that it's more rotational and less steep. This will help correctly move your weight from your back foot and thigh in your backswing to your front foot through impact, and bring your clubhead into impact more from the inside.

133

HOW TO AIM WHERE YOU WANT TO HIT IT
My range drill gets your club and body pointed in the right direction
By PGA Tour player Jim Furyk

I always—always!— hit practice balls with clubs on the ground. This is the only way to find out if your aim is off. You can't do it on your own. Here's my sure-fire method.

STEP 1
Point a club at your target [club 1]. Lay a second club [club 2] a foot to the inside.

STEP 2
Place a third [club 3] where your toes will be and parallel to the other two.

STEP 3
Remove club 1 and set a ball in its place. Then step into the shot. Perfect alignment.

THE IRON GRID:

21 ANSWERS TO YOUR SWING QUESTIONS

The best advice from the best teachers and pros in the game

	Top 100 Teacher **MARTIN HALL**	*PGA Tour player* **SERGIO GARCIA**	*Top 100 Teacher* **MITCHELL SPEARMAN**
Q How can I hit my irons straighter?	**134** **Make left-arm-only swings** with your right hand pressed against your left elbow. Apply pressure the whole way. You should feel a strange sensation as you swing through impact: your left elbow turning down—not folding up. Goodbye, slice.	**137** Plant your left foot on your downswing. This keeps your **lower body in control** for expert strikes. 	**140** **Keep your head centered over the impact area** (nose over the ball as you make contact). This allows you to make your swing as wide as possible on the target side of the ball (just like you should on your backswing) so you can release fully and square up the face at the bottom of your swing.
Q What's the iron-swing basic I can't live without?	**135** **Hide your left knee behind your right knee**—a person watching you from across your target line shouldn't see your left knee and upper left leg when you reach your finish. This helps you transfer all of your weight to your left side during your downswing, as you should.	**138** I like to feel that **80% of my weight** is on my left foot as I swing into my finish. In fact, you should feel like your weight is on the outside of your left foot (left instep slightly off the ground), with your hips facing the target and your right shoulder "chasing" after the ball.	**141** Swing into your release with **level hips and steep shoulders**. Notice how much lower my right shoulder is compared to my left—it's working under my chin, not in front of it.
Q What's a good swing thought I can bring to the course to hit better irons?	**136** Imagine that the fingertips of your right hand are touching the flagstick shortly into your follow-through. This forces **your right arm to extend out toward the target**, which in turn lengthens your left arm and promotes a full release.	**139** Keep your forward bend toward the ball as long as you can (see how the bend in the **right side of my torso makes a "C"?**). 	**142** Imagine **giving the ball a big slap with your right hand**, and continuing the slap in your release. This taps hidden speed in your swing, and creates great arm extension past the ball.

PGA Tour Player	*PGA Tour player*	*Top 100 Teacher*	*Top 100 Teacher*
MIKE BENDER	**HUNTER MAHAN**	**BRADY RIGGS**	**JOHN ELLIOTT, JR.**

143 Take a cross-handed grip with your left hand low. Swing the club back to waist height, and then swing down to your impact position and stop. This gives you the sensation of **your right arm being under your left**, which means the club is swinging correctly from the inside and is on plane.

146 Keep the center of your chest directly over the ball when you make your backswing. **Turning while keeping your chest in place** eliminates swaying and the likelihood of fat contact.

149 Swing with your right foot on a tee marker. Push off the marker and get your weight moving forward.

Exaggerate it so that you lift your right foot off the ground. **You'll never hit it fat again.**

152 Stick a tee in the rear end of the grip on your 5-iron and swing. Try to point the tee immediately at the ground as you begin your downswing. **This narrows your downswing arc** so you can strike the ball with the handle leading the clubhead.

144 Draw a line in the sand about 5 feet long. Using your left hand only, swing across the line, blasting out several divots in front of it. The object is to hit the sand and stop, so that **the grip stays ahead of the clubhead.** This is the forward shaft lean you need at impact when you hit any iron from the fairway.

147 As you take the club away, **feel as though your arms and hands are simply coming along for the ride** as you wind up with your upper body and hips. This gives you the greatest potential energy.

150 From the top, **lead your swing with your right elbow—feel like it's pulling everything down to the ball.** This is a good way to flatten the shaft and stop swinging over the top.

153 Set up a row of tees behind the ball and hit the ball without disturbing the tees. You'll get sufficiently steep in no time.

145 Imagine you're holding a bucket of range balls. Your goal on your backswing is to **spill the balls out gradually over your right shoulder.** That gives you a good idea of proper rotation and staying on plane.

148 Feel like you're **leaning your body toward the target** as you start down. Leaning gets your weight going forward like it should, and it also does an excellent job of keeping your club from falling off plane.

151 Imagine you're hurling a bag of range balls out in front of you. You'll get max distance when you swing your arms around your left shoulder while releasing the bag. Perfect for your swing.

154 If you have trouble creating crisp contact, **imagine that you're trying to strike the ball with the back of your left hand.** If you think about this while trying to hit down, you'll get the ball-first, turf-second contact you need.

ADD CONSISTENCY TO YOUR IRON GAME
How to make your best swings time and again and control distance and trajectory

155

LEAN TOWARD THE TARGET
Straighten up in your finish to stop poor shots and back pain

By Brady Riggs

Leaning away from the target in your finish position *[below, left]* is the fast way to produce weak shots that leak to the right, miss your targets and place undue stress on your back. No athletic motion moves weight away from the target, and this is doubly true for the golf swing. Feel like you're leaning toward the target in your finish *[below, right]*, with your right side fully extended from the toes in your right foot to the tip of your right shoulder. It helps if you think about moving your right shoulder closer to the target than your left as you end your swing. This move not only makes it easier to square the clubface, it takes pressure off your back so you can play pain-free.

Leaning away from the target causes back pain and poor shots.

Leaning toward the target ensures a purer strike and a pain-free swing.

Point the grip toward the ground as soon as your hands reach waist height in your backswing.

157

STOP COMING UP SHORT
Get in touch with the real distance you hit your scoring clubs
By Tim Mahoney

How many times have you missed the green with a short iron? Frustrating, I know. But this is the bane of most amateurs' existence—you pick the club you think will give you 150 yards, not the one you can hit 150 yards consistently. To alleviate this problem, create a distance grid like the one pictured here to discover just how far you hit each of your short irons. Chart ten shots at the range with each club and—this is important—eliminate the longest two. Getting these high extremes out of your mind (i.e., the ones you generate only occasionally), can help you better dial in your distances.

MY DISTANCE CHART			
Shot	7-iron	8-iron	9-iron
1	~~174~~	~~160~~	122
2	~~172~~	140	130
3	159	~~158~~	124
4	155	148	125
5	160	139	125
6	145	141	131
7	152	142	~~138~~
8	144	144	~~140~~
9	149	138	122
10	148	141	127
AVG	151.5	141.6	125.6
AVG*	155.8	145.1	128.4

*Average using extremes

156

THE EASY WAY TO ADD SPEED
A tee is all you need
By Tim Mahoney

Slow swings are stiff swings, and they're powered by a single lever: your arms. Add a second lever by correctly hinging (power storage) and unhinging (power release) your wrists. Cock them earlier—try to point the butt end of the grip at the grass as soon as your hands reach hip height (put a tee in the hole in the grip for a better visual). From here, swing your arms and turn your body to the top. Now, all of your levers are loaded for speed.

SIX TOP 100 TEACHERS ON:
HITTING EVERY IRON FARTHER
Follow these easy tips to add speed and yards and bring any green into range

158
Brad Brewer says
REACH OUT IN YOUR FOLLOW-THROUGH

Take your address position, then remove your left hand from the grip and extend your left arm toward the target with your left thumb facing the sky. Notice as you do this **how your left hip automatically rotates slightly open—the exact position it needs to be in when you strike the ball.** Now swing the club with your right hand and rejoin your hands on the handle. Do this by rotating your hips even more toward the target and shifting your weight into your left thigh and foot.

159
Mitchell Spearman says
LOOK UP TO LAUNCH HIGHER

Take your normal setup but position the ball slightly forward in your stance. Now lift your head up and pick out a cloud or other spot high in the sky directly above your line. Notice as you do this how **your right shoulder drops and your left shoulder rises,** with your spine naturally bending away from the target. This is the exact posture you need to hit the ball higher and farther. When you look back down at the ball, hold the same body position you had when you were looking up at the sky and swing away.

160
Dom DiJulia says
ADD SOME HIP POWER

It's essential to turn your hips enough so you can create a balanced stance at the top of your backswing. To find the correct amount of hip turn, begin your swing and stop when your club is parallel to the ground in your backswing. If a person directly behind you on your toe line can't see your left knee pop out from behind your right knee, you haven't turned your hips enough. The right amount of turn should **allow the person behind you to see your left knee,** and you should feel balanced and stable.

161

Chuck Winstead says
GET YOUR HANDS ABOVE THE CLUBHEAD

The end of your swing has just as much to say about your motion as anything else, and one of the most telling is the relationship between your hands and the clubhead. Ideally **you want a "high finish," with your hands above your head and the clubhead below your hands.** If you're high at the finish, it means you were low (shallow) at the bottom, which is especially key for the longer irons in your bag and if you're guilty of taking too much dirt before the ball at impact.

162

Paul Marchand says
START DOWN WITH A BUMP

When you start your downswing by turning, your swing immediately switches to an outside-in path, even if you were in perfect position at the top. This cut-swing path is the one that gives you your slice or, in the event you square the face, a vicious pull. Instead, at the top, feel like you're sitting down on a chair that's just beneath your rear end and slightly to your left. Use your legs to push your feet into the ground and **move your left hip toward the target.** It's a subtle move, but it works.

163

Paul Trittler says
LIFT YOUR LEFT FOOT FOR MORE TURN

Make your normal backswing and hold it at the top. Now, raise your left foot a few inches off the ground. Notice how this **frees you up to turn a few degrees more**. That's because all of your weight—and the stress that comes with it—went to your right foot. Use a variation of this drill during play. Instead of raising your left foot, roll it to the right and lift your heel slightly. Feel like you're pushing off with your big toe and moving your weight into your right foot.

BACK TO BASICS

If you're struggling to hit solid irons, make sure you have these three setup fundamentals solidly in place

164

HOW TO FIX A FAULTY SETUP
A magazine is all you need
By Carol Preisinger

It happens every time you address the ball: You're not sure how far apart your feet should be, where to position your hands, or where to play the ball in your stance. The solution? Lay a magazine on the ground with both covers face up and follow the checkpoints below.

1. HAND/BALL POSITION
Set the ball even with the magazine's center and set your hands above the spine. You should see a slight lean in the shaft toward the target. Also, check that your hands are over the bottom edge of the magazine.

2. STANCE WIDTH
Take your address with a mid- or long-iron. Set the instep of your right foot even with the edge of the front cover and your left instep with the edge of the back cover. This is the perfect stance width for an iron.

3. POSTURE
Bend from your hips with a flat back until your eyes are over the top edge of the mag. This settles you into the correct posture for an iron. You don't want your head too far out in front of your toes, nor do you want to stand straight up.

165

STOP SLICES AT THE START
Kink in your right side to straighten your shots
By Michael Breed

If you're like most slicers, you're setting up with your upper body over your left foot *[left photo]*. This angles your spine toward the target and places your head in front of the ball. A setup like this will almost definitely lead to a reverse pivot and a swing path that brings the club from out to in. Instead, get your upper body over your right foot at address *[right photo]*, with your spine tilted slightly away from the target. This places your head behind the golf ball and lowers your right shoulder. You know you're doing it right if the left side of your body forms more of a reverse "k" than a straight line.

166

HOW TO NAIL YOUR STANCE WIDTH
Take a walk to see how far you should spread your feet at address
By Mark Hackett

The sure-fire way to find your correct stance width is to simply take a relaxed walk. The length of your stride during a comfortable walk is typically the same as what your stance width should be for a dynamic motion like making a golf swing. Stand where you are, walk a few paces and stop with your right foot ahead of your left. Now pivot to the left a full 90 degrees—this is how you should feel at address.

LEARN FROM THE BEST:

MAHAN'S MOVE FOR SHARP IRONS

Solid advice from one of the game's premier ballstrikers

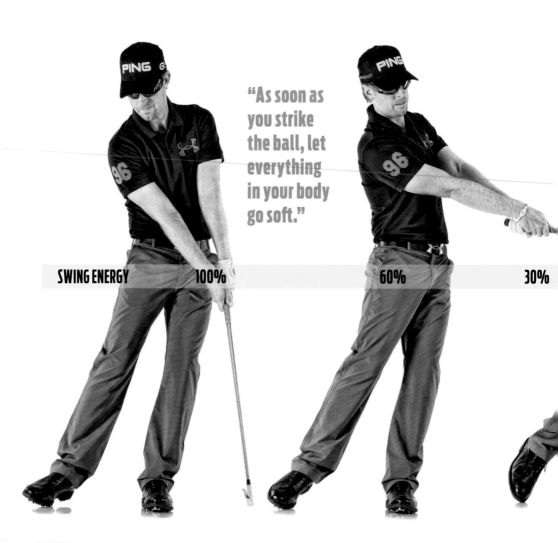

"As soon as you strike the ball, let everything in your body go soft."

SWING ENERGY · · · 100% · · · 60% · · · 30%

SMOOTH
**When your finish
is sufficiently
soft, your arms
should be able
to drop in front
of you due
to gravity.**

0%

167

MAKE YOUR FINISH
A SOFT ONE
Add accuracy—and look
cool doing it
By PGA Tour player Hunter Mahan

If you're one of those players
who tends to fall backward
or forward after impact, or
lean to the left or right so far
that you lose your balance,
this tip is for you. After you
strike the ball, let everything
in your body go soft. You
should go from swinging
your arms as fast as you can
through impact to immediately
feeling like only momentum is
pulling them into your finish. I
strive to make the end of my
swing so soft that my hands
and arms automatically fall
in front of my chest while I'm
tracking the ball in its flight.

If your swing energy is at
100 percent capacity at impact,
you want to get it to zero by the
time your hands reach shoulder
height in your follow-through.
Finishing soft like this allows
you to maintain better balance
and control. Try it a few times
and see how easy it is to keep
your weight balanced over your
left foot and to get your body to
face the target. This is all good
news for your swing. Plus, you'll
look a lot cooler in your finish
than when you're struggling
to stay on your feet.

SHORT GAME

You missed the green and now need to get up and down to keep a big number off your scorecard. With the following 62 tips, moves and drills, you'll get it to tap-in range every time.

168

THE BEST ADVICE FOR YOUR SHORT GAME

Whether you're hitting a pitch or a chip, keep your shoulders level at address

By Todd Sones

The problem most amateurs have when hitting short shots is failing to control the path that the clubhead takes into impact, which should always be descending when you're hitting shots around the green. In other words, the bottom of your swing arc should occur under or beyond the ball, not before it. The trick to producing the right kind of arc is to set up for it in your address. A simple tweak in a few positions will round you into form in no time.

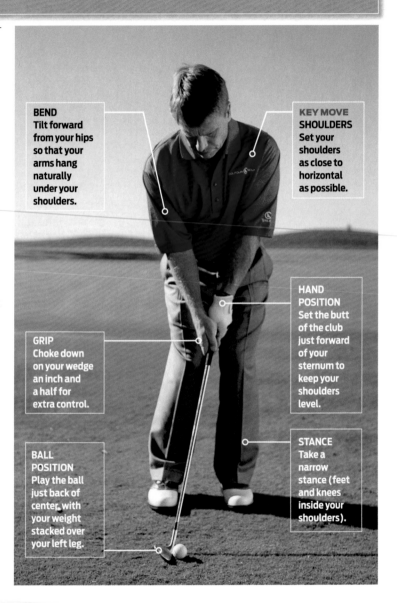

BEND
Tilt forward from your hips so that your arms hang naturally under your shoulders.

KEY MOVE
SHOULDERS
Set your shoulders as close to horizontal as possible.

HAND POSITION
Set the butt of the club just forward of your sternum to keep your shoulders level.

GRIP
Choke down on your wedge an inch and a half for extra control.

STANCE
Take a narrow stance (feet and knees inside your shoulders).

BALL POSITION
Play the ball just back of center, with your weight stacked over your left leg.

HOW TO PITCH IT HIGH OR LOW

Double your shot options with a *few easy tweaks* By Todd Sones

The bad news: Your pitch-shot arsenal is a one-trick pony—not good for meeting the demands of most courses. The good news: You can pitch it high or low on demand by changing your setup and pointing the toe of your club either up or down in your backswing. Here's how.

169
PITCH IT LOW: POINT THE TOE DOWN

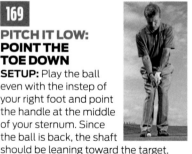

SETUP: Play the ball even with the instep of your right foot and point the handle at the middle of your sternum. Since the ball is back, the shaft should be leaning toward the target. Check that your shoulders are level.

SWING: As you swing back, point the toe toward the ground [photo, above]. As you do, hinge your right wrist back instead of up so that the clubhead moves just inside your hands. Hit the shot by turning your body and club at the same pace.

170
PITCH IT HIGH: POINT THE TOE UP

SETUP: Position the ball just forward of center and again check that the handle is pointing at your sternum and that your shoulders are level. Since the ball is forward, the shaft should sit close to vertical.

SWING: Hinge your wrists up and rotate the clubface open [photo above]. This will give your shot the height it needs. You'll know you're doing it correctly if the toe of the club points up and the club is outside your hands.

HOW TO PITCH WITH PRECISION
Follow the advice on these pages to knock it stiff from tricky distances and lies

CHANGE YOUR SETUP TO MATCH THE LIE
Getting this right allows you to handle anything the course throws at you
By Mike LaBauve

Before attempting any pitch shot, examine your lie. In most cases your ball will be sitting up in the fairway, sitting slightly down in the first cut of rough, or submerged in sizable rough. Each of these lies requires a certain type of pitch swing to ensure the cleanest contact possible. You won't have to change your swing mechanics, just your setup to offset the effects of the grass.

171
If the ball is sitting up
(all of the ball sits above the grass)
Play the ball in the spot where your swing bottoms out

This gives you the cleanest strike since you don't have to worry about interference from the grass. If you don't know where your swing bottoms out, make a practice swing and look for the scuff mark on the grass. The scuff is the bottom of your arc.

172
If the ball is sitting in slight rough
(3/4 of the ball sits above the grass)
Play the ball behind the spot where your swing bottoms out

Position the ball off the instep of your right foot and set your hands in front of your zipper so that the shaft leans toward the target. This encourages ball-first, turf-second contact— a must from heavy grass.

173
If the ball is in deep rough
(1/2 of the ball sits above the grass)
Play the ball forward of the spot where your swing bottoms out

Move the ball toward your left foot, but keep your hands in front of your zipper so that the shaft leans slightly *away* from the target. This puts all the loft of the club to work and gives you the largest possible clubface area with which to make contact.

174
TIGHTEN UP YOUR PITCH SWING
A tee helps you keep your hands ahead of the club through impact
By Dr. Gary Wiren

Stick a tee through the hole on the top of your grip, address a ball and make what you feel is a solid 50-yard pitch. Hold your finish with your hands at waist height (any higher and you will have hit the shot too far). Where is the tee pointing?

If the tee is pointing to the left side of your torso, then you correctly kept your hands ahead of the clubhead and used your body—not your hands—to hit the shot. If the tee is pointing at your stomach, then you flipped your hands or stopped turning your body through impact. You won't even need to look at the tee—your poor technique will show up in your results.

175
HOW TO PITCH IT EXTRA CLOSE
Make a "level" swing for better results
By Tim Mahoney

The best advice I can give you to help your short game is to make your backswing equal to or shorter than your through-swing. If you do the opposite (long backswing, short through-swing), you'll decelerate through the hitting zone and catch the shot fat or thin.

176
HOW TO HIT AN EXPERT FLOP
This high-rising pitch is a real game-saver
By Mike Davis

Grab your lob wedge and set up with the ball positioned between the center of your stance and your left foot, and tilt the shaft away from the target. This aggressive reverse shaft lean adds loft to your club without requiring you to open the face. Use your regular full pitch swing but keep the handle behind the ball at impact. *Voila!*—Instant flop.

SIX TOP 100 TEACHERS ON:

PITCHING PERFECT
The best advice to knock it stiff from short range

177
Nancy Quarcelino says
KEEP THE CLUBHEAD LOW

Your shots typically release and roll well past the cup. Not good when you're looking to stop the ball close to the hole. Fix this problem by maximizing the time the ball spends in contact with the clubface. No, don't slow down your swing. **Just keep the clubhead low all the way through the shot.** When the club stays low to the ground through impact, the ball runs up the clubface and contacts more grooves, creating maximum spin.

178
John Elliott, Jr. says
ROLL AND LIFT YOUR RIGHT ANKLE

Once you complete your pitch backswing, roll your right ankle toward the target, then lift your right heel slightly off the ground. **This subtle bit of downswing footwork gives you the correct amount of weight shift** and turn you need to catch the ball crisp.

179
Bill Forrest says
STAY ON YOUR LEFT SIDE

Pretend you're balanced on a small seesaw. At address, the seesaw should tilt to the left. This means your weight is perfectly positioned so you can hit down on the ball and catch it clean. Practice this by hitting shots with an empty plastic water bottle under your right foot. Use the bottle to remind you to shift your weight over to your left leg. **Shifting your weight forward and keeping it there during your stroke** correctly positions the bottom of your swing arc under the ball.

180

Steve Bosdosh says
LET GRAVITY DO THE WORK

Make practice pitch swings using a dumbbell. Sense how heavy your arms feel at address and how it's impossible to move them quickly when you begin your swing. That teaches you to **make a smooth, unhurried backswing**—an absolute must for good tempo. On the downswing, allow the weight to fall in response to gravity without adding any extra force. On the course, replace the heavy feel of the dumbbell with the weight of your club and again use gravity to pull your arms down into impact.

181

Dana Rader says
KEEP YOUR ARMS CONNECTED

Place a towel under each armpit and take your normal pitching stance. Try to hit 20-yard pitches without the towels falling to the ground. Keeping the towels in place trains you to **connect the turning motion of your torso with the back-and-forth movement of your hands and arms.** If you lift your arms in your backswing without turning your torso to the right, or slap at the ball through impact without turning toward the target, one or both of the towels will drop.

182

Brian Mogg Says
SPEED UP AND STOP TO MAKE IT SIT

Everyone likes to hit pitches that take one good hop after hitting the green and then grab the green harder than a miner's handshake. The secret to doing this is to hinge your wrists quickly on your backswing, bring the club back down to the ball as fast as you can with your hands, and **make an abrupt finish.** The faster you accelerate and then stop, the more the ball will run up your clubface and grab in the grooves. That groove-grab produces spin.

NEW WAYS TO CHIP
Try these Top-100 tips to snuggle the ball close when you miss on your approach

183
HINGE THEN TURN
It's the easy way to get crisp contact
By Tim Mahoney

The two most common chip errors are locking the arms and becoming too rigid, or making a backswing that's much too long. These are critical mistakes that destroy the quality of your contact in a heartbeat. The 4-step technique at right eliminates these problems in an instant, and it will help you pitch the ball closer to the hole more often.

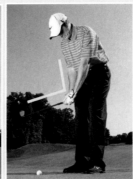

1: SETUP
Assume your normal setup, but make sure your hands are close to your thighs. Feel like your arms and club are connected to your body.

2: HINGE
Hinge your wrists back without rotating your body or turning your shoulders. Just hinge (more for longer shots, less for shorter shots).

3: TURN
Now simply turn your body forward. This should drop the clubhead directly down onto the ball, giving you crisp, ball-first contact.

4: HOLD ON
Don't re-hinge your wrists. Allow your arms to straighten so that the clubshaft is in line with your left arm. This guards against flipping.

184
USE A CLAW GRIP
This special hold stops flippy wrists
By Kellie Stenzel

Instead of placing your right hand below your left, simply wrap it around your left hand with your right thumb directly over your left thumb. No part of your right hand should touch the grip. Now, make your chipping stroke. This right-over-left-hand grip removes your right arm from your stroke, making your chip swing a left-arm-dominated motion. This is a good thing, since it's critical that your left arm never stop moving through the shot.

185

LOOK AT THE TARGET

It's the easy way to increase your chipping touch

By Laird Small

Practice chipping while looking at the target, not the ball. When you focus on the target, you're more apt to turn your body toward the target in your follow-through— an absolute must.

186

CHIP WITH YOUR LEGS

Add a little lower-body action for max control

By Don Kotnik

On the way back to the ball, push your right knee toward the target. This extra bit of lower-body action makes your overall move much smoother.

187

STEP ON THE CLUBFACE

The pro way to pick the right chipping club

By Shawn Humphries

Here's an easy way to figure out the trajectory of a chip with any club. Lay the club along the ground with the clubface up and the shaft pointing toward your target. Now step down on the clubface until the back of the club is flat against the ground. The angle that the shaft rises to is the trajectory of the shots you'll produce with that club.

188

KEEP THE CLUBFACE OPEN

It's the secret to hitting high, soft short shots

By Mike Perpich

When you need to chip the ball over a hazard and stop it quickly once it hits the green, keep the clubface pointing at the sky from setup to finish. Don't release the clubhead like toe over heel like you do on your regular full swing. That will subtract loft and likely give you too much power on the shot.

189

LEAN THE HANDLE FORWARD

Make a lowercase "y" for solid chips

By Tim Mahoney

Notice that when you take your chipping setup how your arms and club form a lowercase "y." You need to maintain this arrangement at impact and throughout your swing. This guarantees that you'll strike the ball cleanly. When you allow the clubhead to pass your hands, you're looking at thin or fat contact.

ADD CONSISTENCY TO YOUR CHIP GAME
These final touches give you the confidence to pull off your best chips on every attempt

4 WAYS TO HIT THE PERFECT CHIP
Check your impact to create solid short shots
By Todd Sones

Your setup and technique are correct if your impact position looks like this:

190
CLUBHEAD LOW
Compare the height of the ball with the height of the clubhead: The ball is high and the clubhead is still very low to the ground. This proves that a downward strike—not an upward flip—gets the ball rolling up the clubface and into the air.

191
WRIST FLAT
You won't chip well if you flip your hands through impact or bend your wrists. Your left wrist should be as flat as possible. If you have trouble keeping your left wrist from breaking down, try using your putting grip.

192
TOE CLOSED
Although your hands should be passive and your left wrist straight, they do need to rotate so that the club turns over on its heel through impact. Try to smoothly rotate the toe of the club toward your target (don't jerk it) as you swing through the impact area.

193
WEIGHT FORWARD
At address, distribute the majority of your weight over your left foot and, more importantly, keep it there throughout your stroke. If you hang back on your right side, you'll swing up into impact—a big-time chip no-no.

194

HOW TO STOP HITTING CHIPS FAT
Set your left wrist flat at address
By Mike Adams

Take your normal chipping-address position and look at your left wrist. If you can see wrinkles in the fold of your wrist, you've created too much of an angle between the shaft and your arms. This is fine when you're swinging the club full because it sets your swing plane up on an arc, but when chipping, you want your motion to be as linear (i.e., straight-back-and-through) as possible. When you set up, stand close enough to the ball so that you remove the up-and-down fold in your left wrist. You shouldn't see any wrinkles below the base of your left thumb. This sets your club on a more upright lie and encourages a back-and-through motion.

Remove the fold in your wrists.

195

FEEL YOUR WAY TO PERFECT SHORT SHOTS
This imaging technique really works
By Mike LaBauve

On the range, instead of hitting a ball toward a target, toss one underhand and see how close you can get. Odds are you'll land it right on the money because your eyes tell your body exactly how hard to toss the ball to cover the distance it's calculated, and you've learned to trust your eyes. Start thinking of your short shots as soft, underhand tosses. Make the same-sized motion you'd use to toss the ball to the target. The images are powerful—if you want to hit a low shot, picture a low toss; if you need to get the ball into the air, picture a high toss.

SHORT-GAME SHOTMAKING

Go from bogey to par and par to birdie by increasing your short-game arsenal with 5 new plays

HOW TO HIT 5 PERFECT SHORT SHOTS

This simple shot arsenal will get you close from the majority of greenside lies

By Bill Forrest

You're 30 yards from the green and need to get up and down. You've been in this situation before, and almost always pulled the wrong club or hit the wrong kind of shot. An easy-to-remember repertoire of shots would help, and here's how to get it. All you need to store in your memory bank are two setups and three swings, then pull them up to generate five different trajectories with specific amounts of carry and roll.

THE SETUPS

A: CHIP ADDRESS
Play the ball back in your stance and set your hands in front of your zipper (shaft leaning forward).
B: PITCH ADDRESS
Play the ball in the middle of your stance. The shaft should sit nearly vertical.

HOW TO HIT EACH SHOT

Combine the right club with the right setup *[below left]* and one of the three swings *[right]* to snuggle the ball close. Before attempting these shots, stand behind the ball and draw a picture in your mind of the trajectory that would work best for the situation. See the ball carry in the air and roll out to the cup once it hits. Get a real sense of the perfect shot shape first, then make your selections.

196
STANDARD PITCH
Club: LW *Setup:* B
Swing: No. 2
Use it: When you need to carry the ball onto the green or just short of it, and then make it check so it doesn't roll past the hole.

197
LOW RUNNING CHIP
Club: 7-iron *Setup:* A
Swing: No. 1
Use it: When you have lots of green to work with, or are playing to an elevated tier.

198
LOFTED PITCH
Club: LW *Setup:* B
Swing: No. 3
Use it: When you have to carry an obstacle, or there's little green to land the ball between the fringe and flagstick.

199
STANDARD CHIP
Club: PW *Setup:* A
Swing: No. 1
Use it: When you have less green to work with, and there aren't any obstacles between you and the green.

200
LOFTED CHIP
Club: LW *Setup:* B
Swing: No. 1
Use it: When you need to loft the ball onto the green, but you still want it to run once it hits.

THE SWINGS

No 1:
None-None
(No hinge back, no hinge through)

Use this for each of the low chip shots. Make more of a putting stroke than a chip stroke using the same pace both back and through. Hold your wrists firm on both sides of the ball, and keep your hands below your belt line.

No. 2:
Some-None
(Medium hinge back, no hinge through)

Hinge your wrists on your backswing, and unhinge them coming back down. This gives your shot height so you can carry the ball farther and control the roll. Once you make impact, keep your wrists firm and finish low.

No. 3:
More-More
(Full hinge back, full hinge through)

To generate max carry with little roll you need to hinge your wrists on both sides of the ball. This kind of wrist action puts maximum loft on the shot, allowing you to carry the ball almost the full distance to the pin.

HOW TO STIFF YOUR WEDGE SHOTS
Dominate from 100 yards and in with full, half and specialty wedge swings

201

THE PRO WAY TO HIT YOUR WEDGES CLOSE
Do what I do: attach your left arm to your chest
By PGA Tour player Dustin Johnson

When you're left with a full wedge to the green, make sure that your left arm stays as close to your chest as possible as you swing the club to the top. This is especially important if you're a tall player like me, where it's easy to lift the club up and get laid off. At address, I'll often set my left arm close to my upper body to remind me to maintain that connection. When I do, I almost always hit the shot I want.

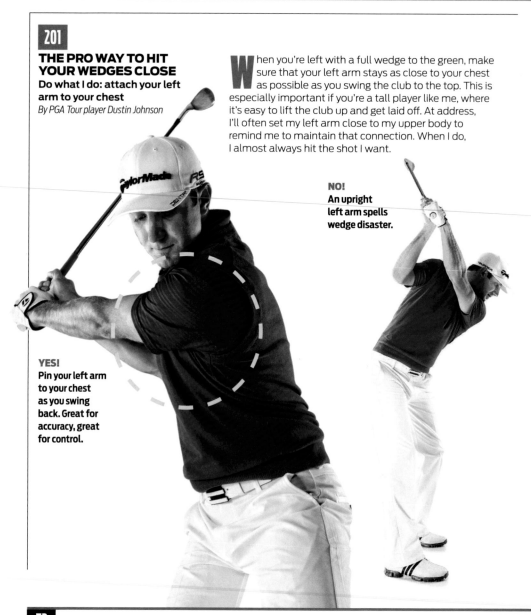

NO!
An upright
left arm spells
wedge disaster.

YES!
Pin your left arm
to your chest
as you swing
back. Great for
accuracy, great
for control.

HIT EVERY YARDAGE ON THE MONEY
A new wedge system allows you to automatically subtract yards without changing your swing
By Mike Adams

202

TO SUBTRACT 1 DISTANCE UNIT

Move your left foot back so that the toe is even with the ball of your right foot **OR...**
Narrow your stance by two clubhead widths **OR...**
Drop your hands to the middle of the grip.

203

TO SUBTRACT 2 DISTANCE UNITS

Move your left foot back so that the toe is even with the instep of your right foot **OR...**
Narrow your stance by three clubhead widths **OR...**
Drop your hands to the bottom of the grip.

204

TO SUBTRACT 3 DISTANCE UNITS

Move your left foot back so that the toe is even with the heel of your right foot.

Hit 10 balls with every wedge in your bag to determine your **Distance Reduction Unit,** which is the number of yards that one setup change from the first row on this page will subtract from each of your wedges. To do this, divide the difference in yardage between any two wedges by the difference in loft between the same two clubs. So, for example, your SW is 12 yards longer than your LW, and your LW has four degrees more loft. Divide 12 by 4, which gives you a Distance Reduction Unit of 3 yards.

THREE THOUGHTS FOR EXPERT WEDGES

Call up these when you're faced with a short approach on the course

205

USE NATURAL ROTATION

It makes your wedge swing a free-flowing motion

By PGA Tour player Sergio Garcia

When I hit my wedges I like to feel my club rotating open, so that the toe points at the sky halfway back in my takeaway. I'll reverse the process through impact, so that the toe points to the sky on the target side of my swing. This gives me a smooth, accelerating release that almost always produces a clean, centered strike. Of course, it's easy to confuse opening the face with twisting your wrists, a move that whips the clubhead behind you. The feeling you're after is a gentle rolling of your forearms. You'll know you're doing it correctly if the logo on the back of your club points out in front of you, not toward the sky.

206

SWING YOUR WEDGES AT 90 PERCENT
You'll get the same distance and better contact
By PGA Tour player Camilo Villegas

It's okay to swing longer clubs, like your driver, at full speed because you create enough centrifugal force to keep your body in good position during the swing. But since the shaft on your wedge is almost a foot shorter than your driver, it creates much less centrifugal force during your swing. As a result, your body doesn't respond as well to high swing speeds with the shorter club, causing you to slide out of position. Wedge shots are all about accuracy; don't try to swing harder than 90 percent. If that isn't enough to get you to your target, take more club. You'll get better results by swinging easier.

207

FOCUS ON YOUR FINISH
Perfection here means solid results
By Mark Hackett

You know you've made a solid 100-yard wedge swing if you end your swing with a complete finish and in total balance. Notice that I've only slightly raised my right heel—it's not way up like it is when I'm swinging driver. It's a good idea to feel a little flat-footed when swinging your wedge to help with your control.

THE SHORT IRON GRID:

21 ANSWERS TO YOUR WEDGE PLAY QUEST

Everything you wanted to know about your short game but were afraid to ask

	Top 100 Teacher **TIM MAHONEY**	Top 100 Teacher **JOHN ELLIOTT, JR.**	Top 100 Teacher **BILL FORREST**
Q What's the quick way to improve my chipping immediately?	**208** **Keep your hands and clubhead below your waist** in your follow-through. Make a few chip swings and try to mimic the right-side photo below. 	**211** Allow your right leg to kink—it should feel like your right knee is gently moving toward the target as you swing through the impact zone. **The angle of your lower leg should match the shaft at impact.**	**214** This one's easy—**set up with the majority of your weight on your front foot and keep it there.** You can even shift more weight to your front foot on your downswing, but never back.
Q How can I increase my short-game options beyond a standard pitch and chip?	**209** After impact, try to **brush the grass in front of the ball**—it's an easy way to add spin to hop-and-stop chips.	**212** Keep your **right-hand knuckles pointed at the ground after impact.** It's the easy way to add loft to your short shots and make them land soft.	**215** When you need to chip it short, high and soft, keep the face of your wedge from closing down at impact. In your release, **the face of your wedge should look as flat as a pancake.** 
Q What are some good drills I can use to practice my short-shot techniques?	**210** Hit several chips in a row on the practice green **without ever taking your eyes off the ball.** Hear the shot land. If you peek, your contact will suffer.	**213** When you pitch, hold your finish at belt high and **check that the shaft forms a straight line with your right forearm.** That means you're hitting, not flipping.	**216** Hit some practice pitches using only your right arm. Doing this frees up your motion since you have less control of the club, forcing you to **accelerate while turning toward the target.** 

Top 100 Teacher	*Top 100 Teacher*	*Top 100 Teacher*	*Top 100 Teacher*
MARTIN HALL	**SCOTT HACKETT**	**KELLIE STENZEL**	**MARK HACKETT**

217 Get into your address position and cock your head to the left, so that **your left eye is closer to the ground than your right.** Now the bottom of your swing arc is underneath the ball—where it needs to be for solid chip contact.

220 Regardless of how far off the green the ball is sitting, or where the pin is positioned, **try to land every chip one pace on the front edge of the green.** That gives you a baseline for determining the exact amount of carry versus roll for every shot (see tip 222).

223 **If you tend to hit your chips too far,** set your hands near the bottom of the grip so that your right thumb is nearly touching the shaft. This makes your wedge much shorter and reduces the amount of power you can deliver to the ball.

226 Whenever you decide to play the ball back in your stance, remember that the clubface wants to open up and point a little right of where you're aimed. **Rotate the face a few degrees to get it pointing at your target.**

218 To hit a pro-style flop, **lift the last three fingers on your left hand off the grip as you swing though impact.** Removing these fingers allows your clubhead to slide underneath the ball, which adds extra loft to your clubface, helping to launch the ball extra high.

221 Through impact, **swing your arms to the left of the target,** not toward the target.

YES! / NO!

224 Set up with the ball in the middle of your stance and your feet almost touching. This **ultra-narrow stance limits the flexibility in your hips, so you turn less** and cut your backswing short without having to think about it. Good for delicate chips to sloping greens.

227 Moving the ball forward in your stance increases the effective loft. **This will help you add height** so the ball can pop up and sit down almost immediately.

219 Stick a shaft in the ground as shown. Your goal is to make contact without swinging past the shaft, teaching you to **accelerate into the ball, not after.**

222 Use this guide to gauge the right amount of carry vs. roll for landing shots one pace on:
(Carry:Roll):
< 2:1 = LW
2:1 = SW
1:1 = PW
1:2 = 9-iron
1:3 = 8-iron
1:4 = 7-iron
1:5 = 6-iron

225 **Chip with a left-hand-low grip.** This makes it harder to swing your arms and hands away from the target, allowing you to control backswing length on delicate chips.

228 Choke down on the handle in varying amounts, and see how each one gives you a different distance with each of your typical pitch clubs. **When you choke down, be careful to bend your knees.** You don't want to just bend from your hips, since you've lowered the shortened club down to the ground.

TEST YOUR SHORT GAME

This exclusive test tells you where you're making strides and where you need the most work

229

HOW GOOD IS YOUR SHORT GAME?

Pass these skill challenges and you'll be well on your way to establishing a reliable wedge game

By Dave Pelz
Golf Magazine's technical and short-game consultant

There's nothing worse—or more frustrating—than knowing that a part of your game needs work but not really knowing the root of your problems. Here's a systematic way to narrow your "to-do" list so you can concentrate on the areas of your short game that consistently cause you to lose strokes and not waste time practicing moves you already have down pat. You're going to be tested on your ability to hit a variety of short game shots. Don't worry—there are no wrong answers, just a heavy dose of invaluable insight into the golfer you are and the one you want to be.

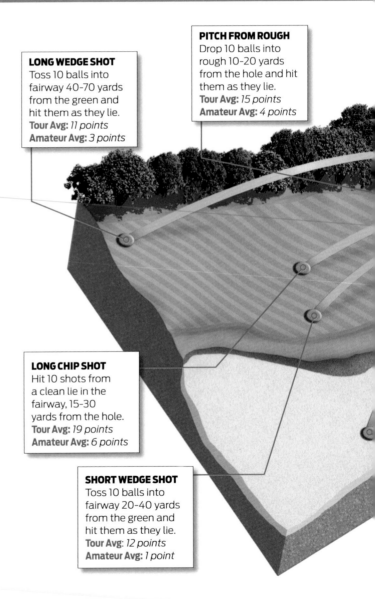

PITCH FROM ROUGH
Drop 10 balls into rough 10-20 yards from the hole and hit them as they lie.
Tour Avg: *15 points*
Amateur Avg: *4 points*

LONG WEDGE SHOT
Toss 10 balls into fairway 40-70 yards from the green and hit them as they lie.
Tour Avg: *11 points*
Amateur Avg: *3 points*

LONG CHIP SHOT
Hit 10 shots from a clean lie in the fairway, 15-30 yards from the hole.
Tour Avg: *19 points*
Amateur Avg: *6 points*

SHORT WEDGE SHOT
Toss 10 balls into fairway 20-40 yards from the green and hit them as they lie.
Tour Avg: *12 points*
Amateur Avg: *1 point*

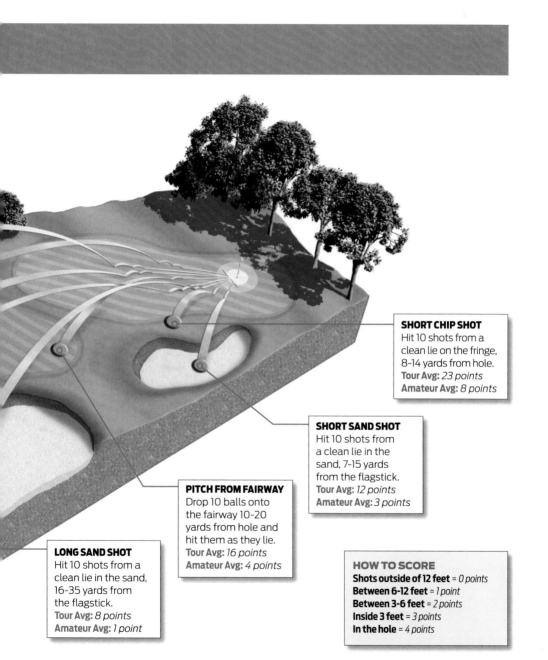

SHORT CHIP SHOT
Hit 10 shots from a clean lie on the fringe, 8-14 yards from hole.
Tour Avg: *23 points*
Amateur Avg: *8 points*

SHORT SAND SHOT
Hit 10 shots from a clean lie in the sand, 7-15 yards from the flagstick.
Tour Avg: *12 points*
Amateur Avg: *3 points*

PITCH FROM FAIRWAY
Drop 10 balls onto the fairway 10-20 yards from hole and hit them as they lie.
Tour Avg: *16 points*
Amateur Avg: *4 points*

LONG SAND SHOT
Hit 10 shots from a clean lie in the sand, 16-35 yards from the flagstick.
Tour Avg: *8 points*
Amateur Avg: *1 point*

HOW TO SCORE
Shots outside of 12 feet = *0 points*
Between 6-12 feet = *1 point*
Between 3-6 feet = *2 points*
Inside 3 feet = *3 points*
In the hole = *4 points*

PUTTING

Improving your putting and limiting the number of strokes you take on the green is the fast way to drop your scores. Try our top tips to start putting the lights out and going low.

230

THE BEST ADVICE FOR YOUR STROKE
Keep your right elbow in and you'll never stray off path
By PGA Tour putting coach Marius Filmalter

My access to computer-generated data on 50,000 putting strokes puts me in a unique position: I know what good putters do and what bad putters don't do. Part of any kind of putting analysis is looking at techniques that generate the best results, and for my money you can't beat keeping your right elbow tucked against the right side of your torso from start to finish. This right-elbow position—something I see over and over again in the good putting strokes that I review—is a key component in swinging your putter back and through on the correct path and with good tempo. When you lose your right elbow/torso connection, the putter rises up off the ground, making it difficult to strike the ball squarely. To stop this from happening, practice the following:

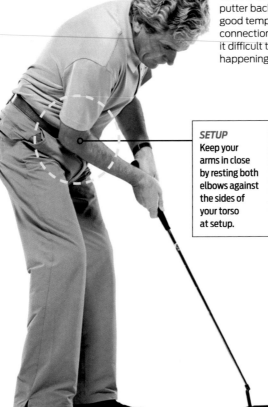

SETUP
Keep your arms in close by resting both elbows against the sides of your torso at setup.

BACKSTROKE
Power the putter back more with your shoulders than with your arms, and keep your right elbow tucked.

FORWARD-STROKE
Again, power the club through more with your shoulders and maintain that right-elbow connection all the way to your finish. Pinning your right elbow like this puts you in better position to trace the correct path.

"5"
Pull the trigger

Count "1"
Step in

Count "2"
Take your stance

Count "3"
Look at your target

Count "4"
Look back at the ball

231

PUTT SMOOTHER IN 5 EASY STEPS
This "freeze-fixing" pre-putt routine has been a hit on Tour
By PGA Tour putting coach Marius Filmalter

You're facing a tricky 6-footer and you just can't *seem...to... pull...the...trigger*. You freeze—a putting malady that takes you out of your natural rhythm and makes executing a smooth stroke impossible. If this sounds like you, copy Aaron Baddeley, who has had another excellent putting year. Aaron steps in, spreads his feet, looks at the hole, the ball, and then he putts. I suggest you count the steps in your head. When you look down, count "1." Count "2" as you look back to the ball, and so on *[photos above]*. Build tempo into this cycle—complete each step in rhythmic time (i.e., don't jump from one step to the next faster or slower than you do for the others). The five-frame cycle is ideal. Anything less and you're probably not giving the putt your best effort; anything longer is treading toward "freezing."

HOW TO ADDRESS EVERY PUTT

Nailing your setup makes it easy to putt on line and make contact in the center of your putterface

4 KEY SETUP POSITIONS

Practice your putting posture by focusing on the four most critical areas

By Todd Sones

Stand up straight with your putter out in front of you as shown. Then rotate your elbows inward and rest them on your rib cage. Tilt forward from your hips until your putter comes to rest under your eyes. Do it right and you'll nail the four key setup positions pictured here.

Start your address check with your putter out in front of you and your elbows set snug against your torso.

232
HANDS UNDER SHOULDERS
This allows your putter to swing back and through naturally on the proper path.

233
EYES OVER THE INSIDE EDGE OF THE BALL
This gives you the best optical view of the target line.

234
SHAFT MATCHES THE FOREARMS
They should form a straight line. If they don't, your putter is too long or short.

235
HIPS OVER HEELS
This sets your weight evenly over your feet so you can stay balanced from start to finish.

236

THE PURE-PUTT GRIP SECRET
Copy this hold for a better stroke and more confidence
By Todd Sones

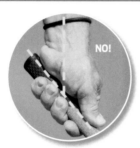

To make your stroke natural and automatic, grip the club diagonally through your palms, not through your fingers. Remember, a putt is not like a full shot, where you want to create an angle between your arms and the club. Instead you want the shaft of the putter directly in line with your forearm and hanging right below your shoulder sockets. By making this small change to your grip, the clubhead will move right into your eyeline, making it much easier to aim consistently and accurately.

238

HOW TO KNOW YOUR AIM IS TRUE
A credit card will tell you in an instant
By Charlie King

You'll need a friend to help with this drill. Set up to a straight 8-foot putt on the green. Have your friend switch the ball for a credit card, placing it as shown. Now, stand back and look down the long edges of the card—lines extending out from these should bracket the cup. If you're off, repeat the drill, but align the card first. Then place a ball on the card and set the face square to the edge of the plastic. This allows you to see what straight really looks like.

237

HOLD YOUR ADDRESS FOR A SMOOTHER STROKE
Maintaining your posture keeps your stroke from falling off path
By Tim Mahoney

ADDRESS

IMPACT

Maintain your lines—the distances from your head, chest, elbows and hands to the ground need to remain intact from start to finish. This allows you to put the purest strike possible on the ball. It's a better swing thought than "keep your body still," which typically invites undue tension and reduces feel.

HOW TO FIND THE RIGHT HOLD

Customizing your grip to match your putter and stroke preferences is the fast track to more one-putts and fewer three-putts

PICK YOUR GRIP

My research on 10 popular holds proves there's a right one for you

By Tom Stickney

We tested* the ten most common alternative grips and discovered that some are better for improving distance control while others are better for directional control. The higher your handicap, the more help you need with distance control—go with a grip that keeps your left wrist from breaking down and changing the shaft angle (which adds or subtracts loft from your putter). If you're a more accomplished player, you probably need to work on fine-tuning your impact position—look for grips that keep the putterface from unduly opening and closing on your forward-stroke. In the following tables, the best overall grip for each handicap group is highlighted in yellow.

Using SAM PuttLab

INTERLOCKING

239

Best used in the hands of a skilled putter, but provides no additional benefit compared to other grips.

Handicap	Impact Aim	Impact Loft
Scratch	0.3° open	-1.6°
10	0.4° closed	+1.2°
18	1.9° closed	+0.8°
25	2.9° open	+0.9°
36	1.8° closed	-0.2°

OVERLAP

240

Provides a similar feel to the full-swing grip—a comfort to high-handicappers who lose touch when they switch to a new grip.

Handicap	Impact Aim	Impact Loft
Scratch	0.2° open	-1.6°
10	0.3° closed	+1.3°
18	1.1° closed	+0.6°
25	1.3° open	+1.0°
36	1.0° open	-0.1°

SPLIT BASEBALL

244

A solid option for higher handicaps, but in the hands of a scratch player it will cause putts to dive into the turf and bounce.

Handicap	Impact Aim	Impact Loft
Scratch	0.6° open	-2.0°
10	0.5° open	+1.2°
18	1.8° open	+0.2°
25	1.1° open	+1.7°
36	0.7° closed	+.4°

LEFT-HAND LOW

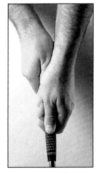

245

An effective grip for keeping the putterface pointed at the target through impact. High handicaps might have difficulty adjusting.

Handicap	Impact Aim	Impact Loft
Scratch	0.4° open	-0.9°
10	0.2° open	+2.0°
18	0.7° closed	+2.4°
25	3.2° open	+0.4°
36	3.3° closed	+2.4°

REVERSE OVERLAP

241

A middle-of-the-pack grip for all handicap levels.

Handicap	Impact Aim	Impact Loft
Scratch	0.5° open	-0.6°
10	0.9° closed	+1.5°
18	2.9° closed	-0.2°
25	2.3° open	+0.5°
36	2.3° closed	+2.1°

REVERSE OVERLAP

242

w/long finger

Helps 25-handicappers keep excess hand action in check but with less distance control.

Handicap	Impact Aim	Impact Loft
Scratch	0.4° open	-2.1°
10	0.5° closed	+1.0°
18	1.7° closed	-0.7°
25	0.7° closed	+1.5°
36	1.8° open	-1.4

BASEBALL

243

Provides too much control for the already skilled hands of a scratch player (shaft leaning forward at impact).

Handicap	Impact Aim	Impact Loft
Scratch	0.8° open	-1.6°
10	0.5° closed	+1.3°
18	1.2° closed	-1.1°
25	2.1° open	+1.2°
36	2.4° open	+1.2°

CLAW

246

Encourages extra shoulder rotation for scratch golfers (closed face), but cures faults typical of mid-range players.

Handicap	Impact Aim	Impact Loft
Scratch	0.4° closed	-1.0°
10	0.1° closed	+0.7°
18	1.0° closed	+0.9°
25	2.1° open	-0.7°
36	0.6° closed	+1.6°

LANGER

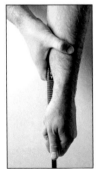

247

Another solid option for the 10-handicapper, a player whose primary fault is excess hand action and poor face control.

Handicap	Impact Aim	Impact Loft
Scratch	0.1° closed	-1.7°
10	0.5° open	+0.6°
18	2.5° closed	-0.1°
25	3.5° open	+0.9°
36	2.7° open	+0.4°

STRONG RIGHT HAND

248

Unlike its role in the full swing, a strong right hand position does very little to control putterface position at impact.

Handicap	Impact Aim	Impact Loft
Scratch	0.9° open	-1.1°
10	0.3° open	+1.6°
18	2.2° closed	-0.1°
25	1.3° open	+0.9°
36	1.6° closed	-2.5°

SIX TOP 100 TEACHERS ON:

SETTING UP TO PUTT YOUR BEST
Putting address and alignment tips from the experts who know best

249

Tim Mahoney says
KEEP YOUR RIGHT WRIST BENT

Get into your putting address position and check that your right wrist is bent back as you set your putterhead next to the ball. Next, make your stroke, thinking of nothing but maintaining the same angle in your right wrist past impact. You should be able to hold this position in your finish. **It's critical that your right wrist never straighten**—if it does, the putterhead will flip past your hands and make centered contact almost impossible.

250

J.D. Turner says
ADJUST BALL POSITION DEPENDING ON BREAK

If your putt breaks left-to-right you're on an uneven lie with the ball below your feet, just like a slice lie in the fairway. Move the ball slightly forward in your stance, off your front foot *[photo, above]*. This will stop you from contacting the ball too soon and missing to the right. **If your putt breaks right-to-left** you're on an uneven lie with the ball above your feet, just like a hook lie in the fairway. Play the ball toward the center of your stance. This will allow you to make contact with the ball earlier, so you don't pull it.

251

Scott Sackett says
GET YOUR EYES OVER THE BALL

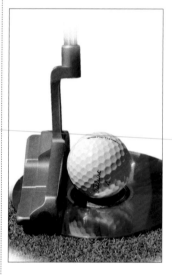

Position a ball in the little hole in the middle of an old music CD, shiny side up. Address the ball as if you were going to putt it and **check where your eyes reflect on the CD.** If your eyes are inside the ball, bend slightly forward from your hips until they move over the middle of the CD. If your eyes are outside the ball, bend slightly back from your hips. Eyes over the ball gives you the best view of the line and stops pull and push strokes in their tracks.

252
Jim Murphy says
PICTURE DRIVING A TEE INTO THE BALL

At address, turn all your thoughts to making solid contact. Imagine that there's a tee attached to the sweet spot of your putter, with the pointed end aimed at your target. **Visualize driving the point on the tee into a dimple in the center of the ball** when you make your stroke. This picture is a good one to help you strike the ball squarely and with the right amount of loft. Even better, you won't have to worry about swinging up into the ball.

253
Tom Stickney says
KEEP YOUR ELBOWS 12 INCHES APART

Studies show that when your elbows are 12 inches apart (with the "pockets" pointing almost straight up), they bend the right amount and put you in **the best position to make a smooth stroke on the correct path.** When they're more than 12" apart, your arms become too tight to make a fluid stroke and you have to raise up to keep your hands on the handle. At less than 12" apart, your posture becomes too hunched—you're likely to raise up during your stroke and push the ball to the right.

254
Paul Marchand says
KEEP YOUR NECK FLAT

Reach around to the back of your neck and find that little bone that protrudes from the base near the top of your back. That's your pivot point. Now, **bend forward so that the bone and the base of your neck are parallel to the ground.** Notice how your arms hang freely and your hands are directly underneath your shoulders. This posture automatically creates the preferred pendulum motion. All you have to do is start your putter back, and it will swing back and through on the path you chose.

HOW TO GROOVE A SOLID STROKE
Keep these moves in mind when you're on the practice putting green honing your technique

255

TRACE THE CORRECT PATH
My stroke test grades your motion, then tells you how to improve it
By PGA Tour putting coach Marius Filmalter

Place a 2 x 4 on the ground and set up to putt a ball with the toe of your putter just barely touching the wood. Now, try to take your putter straight back by keeping the toe in constant contact with the 2 x 4. Feels awful, right? It is. That's because in order to make this kind of stroke you must allow your right elbow to fly out and separate from your body. From this position you have zero chance of striking the ball in the center of your putterface with the correct amount of loft.

Try the test again, but this time swing your putter to the inside on a nice arc, with the toe losing contact with the board. This is the stroke you need to putt your best. Be careful not to rotate your hands to create the arc. Create the arc by turning your shoulders. Practice this drill from time to time to make sure you have enough arc in your stroke—it comes and goes for most players. You can perform this drill against the baseboard on any wall, too.

An arc-like stroke makes it easy to strike the ball squarely and with the correct loft.

A straight-back stroke sounds like a good idea...

...until you see how it forces your right elbow to fly, delofting the putterface.

256
HOW TO SPOT YOUR PUTTING FLAWS
You've got to know what's broken before you can start making repairs
By Scott Munroe

Find a flat section of the green and build the putting station pictured here. Use it to check the following:

FIX YOUR EYE LINE
The line should look like it's slicing the ball in half. This is a setup must.

FIX YOUR BODY AIM
Set your toes even with the string, correctly aiming your body parallel left.

FIX YOUR FACE AIM
Set your putterface perpendicular to the string to feel what it's like to aim the face at the target.

FIX YOUR PATH
Swing your putter slightly inside the string on both sides of the ball.

FIX YOUR IMPACT
Roll the ball between the two tees. If you miss, you know something's wrong with your face position at address.

257
PRACTICE WITH A BELLY PUTTER
This long-shafted model is good for giving your stroke the extra smoothness it needs
By Peter Krause

A belly putter fuels a more rhythmic stroke because it takes your hands and wrists (the moving parts that cause the yips) out of your stroke. Here's how to use it:

1. Hold the grip in the palm of your right hand so the shaft is in line with your right forearm. Your right arm should be hanging fairly relaxed.

2. Hold the top of the grip with your left hand so that your left forearm is parallel with the ground.

3. Stroke with your shoulders while maintaining the angles in your right and left forearms that you established at setup. You should feel like your left shoulder drops down going back and rises up in your follow-through, just like you're sweeping the kitchen floor.

THE PUTTING GRID:

21 ANSWERS TO YOUR PUTTING QUESTION

The best advice from the best teachers in the game

	Top 100 Teacher **EDDIE MERRINS**	Top 100 Teacher **PETER KRAUSE**	Top 100 Teacher **TODD SONES**
Q I don't feel very confident in my setup and aim. What's the easy way to improve my address?	**258** Make sure you're set up to use the loft built into your putter, with your weight evenly distributed and the **handle pointing at or left of your navel.** When you press the shaft forward or set too much weight over your front foot, you take loft off the face, creating a bouncing effect instead of true forward roll.	**261** Get in your setup, take your right hand off the grip and let your right arm hang. If your hand hangs inside the grip, you're standing too far from the putter. **Your right arm should hang even with the handle.**	**264** Pick a spot where you think the apex of the putt (maximum break) will be and examine the putt by looking from behind your ball to that spot. **This gives you a better sense of the true line** and makes it easier to align the face on the line you want the ball to start (toward the apex).
Q I haven't made a putt in a month. What can I do to quickly improve my stroke?	**259** Have a friend step on your ball while you try to putt. At contact, you should feel like you're trying to move the putter through the ball by moving the handle, not the putterhead.	**262** Tap your innate hand-eye control and **aim for the equator of the ball on every putt.** Forget about everything else and focus on the strike point during your next practice sessions. You'll be surprised how quickly the quality of your contact improves.	**265** **Set your hands under your shoulders at address.** This allows them to swing back naturally, without moving outside the target line or inside the target line. Works every time.
Q I would practice my putting more if it wasn't so boring. Are there any good drills to help me keep my focus?	**260** To practice your lag putting, **set a "distance line" past the hole that you must reach on each attempt.** Set the line 1 foot past the hole for every 20 feet of putt length. Get good at this drill, and the longest second putt you'll leave yourself is an easy three-footer, even from 60 feet.	**263** Putt through two tees as shown. This drill fixes your shoulder alignment. If you're open or closed you'll hit one of the two tees.	**266** Rest a club on a tee as shown with a ball placed under the butt end of the grip. Now, make your  stroke. If you knock the club off the tee, **you're flipping your hands through impact.**

PGA Tour Putting Coach	Top 100 Teacher	PGA Tour Putting Coach	Top 100 Teacher
MARIUS FILMALTER	**JON TATTERSALL**	**PAUL HURRION**	**MIKE ADAMS**

267 If you like to take your putter straight back and through, **bend forward more at address.** The taller you stand at setup the more your putter wants to swing back and through on an arc.

270 Copy the left-side photo below, where the **hands are directly opposing one another** instead of facing in different directions.

273 The direction your putterface points at address largely determines where the ball will go, so it's vital that you set your blade perfectly square to the line.

276 The less toe hang on your putter (i.e., the more face-balanced it is), the more you should play the ball back in your stance and bend from your hips at address. **With greater toe hang, the more arc you need in your stroke,** and you create arc by standing taller and playing the ball forward in your stance.

268 **Try humming or whistling while you putt,** keeping time with your backstroke and forward-stroke. You'll get smooth in no time.

271 As you putt, **count "one" going back and "two" as you strike the ball.** This counting trick gives you a smoother tempo so you'll be less likely to manipulate the face open with your hands.

274 Just like it did at address, your **putterface should make a right angle with your intended line, both 2 inches before and 2 inches after impact.** If you're off here you'll put either hook or cut spin on the ball and it will roll offline. This is especially true on slow greens.

277 On uphill putts, take your practice strokes behind the ball. Practice in front of the ball on downhill putts. This allows you to gauge the real distance.

269 This one is good for yippers. Grip your putter using only your thumbs and forefingers. Place your left hand at the top of the handle and your right hand at the very bottom of the grip. Your goal is to keep the putter from "wobbling," in which the head passes the handle. The only way to do it is to **maintain constant speed.**

272 Putt underneath a string with your eyes closed. Hold the end of your backstroke, open your eyes and check your putterhead.

If it's **slightly inside but still under the string,** you're solid.

275 Make a fluid transition from backstroke to forward-stroke. Try to almost **pause your stroke before starting back to the ball.**

278 Place two balls side-by-side flush against your putterface and strike the putt. If the ball closest to the toe section of your putter rolls farther than the ball closest to the heel, you should use a toe-weighted putter. If the opposite happens, or both balls travel the same distance, **opt for a face-balanced putter.**

HOW TO SMOOTH OUT YOUR STROKE

These two teacher tricks give your stroke the right pace and the right length to hole every putt imaginable

279

PUTT WITH PERFECT PACE

Find your personal tempo and roll it smooth every time

By Mike Adams

"TICK"

"TOCK"

The pace at which you should swing your putter is the tempo that's wired into your system—it's the personal pace at which you go about most of the motor actions you execute in a day. The easy way to find it is to find a flat section of ground and walk around. Have a friend time you for 45 seconds and count the number of steps you take during that time. At the end of 45 seconds, tally the steps and repeat. Do this five times, then compute your average. That number is a concrete representation of your tempo.

Now, set your personal tempo number on a metronome (there are a number of very good apps for this that you can download and use on your smart phone). Next, anchor two blocks of wood to the green with some tees, setting one outside your right foot and the other where you play the ball in your stance [photos, left]. Take your stance and swing your putter back and forth, striking each block on successive beeps from the metronome. It helps to count "1-2, 1-2" in your head as you strike the blocks in time with the metronome. After a while, move the block on your right closer to the impact block, and then even farther away. Regardless of the stroke length you're practicing, try to maintain the same "tick-tock" pace for all putts from all lengths.

280

LAG ANY DISTANCE, ANY TIME
Build a stroke-length inventory to putt with confidence from all corners of the green
By Ted Sheftic

Hit the practice green and find a nice flat spot (you don't need a hole). Settle into your stance and follow these steps:

With this drill you'll learn to putt the ball three distinct distances in about five minutes (just match the distance to the backstroke length). It's the same principle as knowing how far you hit each iron in your bag. When you're caught at distances between the ones in your inventory, fine-tune your stroke by either taking the putter back a little farther or a little shorter.

IMPORTANT: Control putt speed with stroke length, not by speeding up or slowing down your motion.

20-foot stroke

STEP 1
Take the putterhead back to your right toe using your normal tempo and rhythm, and then strike the putt as you normally would. Once the ball stops rolling, walk off the distance (it should be about 18 to 20 feet).

30-foot stroke

STEP 2
Settle into your stance again and make another stroke. This time, take your hands back to your right toe (giving you about 28-30 feet of distance).

40-foot stroke

STEP 3
Make a third stroke. On this one, take your hands outside your right toe. When you walk this one off you'll find that this backstroke length gives you 38 to 40 feet of distance.

GROOVING A TOUR-QUALITY STROKE
These stroke thoughts and practice drills really work

281

Chuck Winstead says
TAP YOUR PUTTER TO START YOUR STROKE

After taking your stance, count off as follows: **1)** Count "ONE" as you lower the putterhead and gently tap the ground behind your ball; **2)** "TWO" as you then raise the putter back off the ground about an inch; and **3)** "THREE" as you tap the ground again and immediately start your backstroke. This one-two-three tap sequence creates a cadence that gives you the right frame of mind and correct sense of rhythm to execute a smooth and symmetrical backstroke and forward stroke on every putt.

282

Michael Breed says
WORK ON LEVELING YOUR STROKE

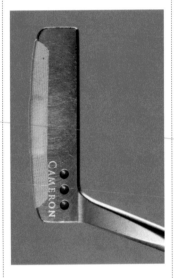

Place a Band-Aid on the bottom third of the putterface as shown above and stroke a few practice putts. Your goal is to strike the ball above the Band-Aid. You'll know when you make contact with the Band-Aid because the putt will feel dead and it will come up short. **Practicing like this forces you to keep the putter level through impact** and, at the very least, to make sure that you don't flip the club up into the ball.

283

Brady Riggs says
LOOK AT THE HOLE WHEN YOU LAG

You're so concerned with your stroke that **you forget about the most critical element of lag putting—distance control.** It's an easy mistake to make, because in golf, you focus your eyes on the ball, not the target. However, this impedes your innate ability to "feel" the distance to the hole. My solution is to look at the hole when you lag. This allows you to focus on the target and forget about your stroke and the ball.

284

Dan Pasquariello says
ROLL A ROLL OF PENNIES

285

Robert Baker says
KEEP YOUR HANDS AHEAD OF THE BALL

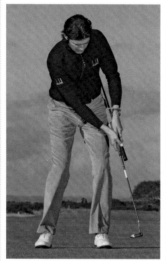

286

Jerry King says
SINK PUTTS WITH BETTER SPEED

Take those pennies you've been saving for a rainy day and fill a coin wrapper, then take the roll to the practice putting green, drop it about three feet from the hole on a flat section of the green and try to putt it into the hole.
If the roll spins to the left, the toe of your putter is catching it first, which means you're closing the putterface through impact.
If the roll spins to the right, the heel of your putter is catching it first, which means you're opening the putterface through impact.

Grip your putter and another club held upside down as shown and make your stroke. The grip of your putter should be slightly ahead of the ball at impact. **Allowing the putterhead to lag this way gives you a smooth, end-over-end roll.** If you lose your lag, the shaft of the second club will press into your left side and the ball will come up short. Overdo the lag and the shaft will come off your left side, and you'll drive the ball into the turf.

Find a straight 10-foot putt and set two tees in the green just wider than a ball's width apart. Place the ball just a sliver inside the tees *[see photo]* so that when you putt you hit the pegs before you hit the ball. As you roll putts from this setup, you'll find that the ball really "pops" out of the gate, even though you can't make a full stroke. By forcing you to "crash" through the tees, **the drill helps you accelerate at impact and roll the ball with ample pace.**

READ GREENS LIKE A PRO
How to gauge break, slope and speed like a cagey veteran

287

BE A GREEN-READING DETECTIVE
All the clues to the break are out in the open
By Todd Sones

While a good course designer will do his best to challenge your green-reading abilities, he'll also leave obvious clues about how the ball will roll on different areas of the green. If you know what to look for, you'll know the general slope of the green even before you get behind your ball.

Putts break away from the clubhouse
Clubhouses are normally built on the highest point on the course. Look for home, and you'll get an idea of the general lay of the land.

Putts break toward water
For obvious drainage reasons, greens will slope toward the nearest body of water. On oceanside courses, don't underestimate the natural roll of terrain toward the sea.

Putts break away from hills
Don't forget the obvious. Putts will break away from greenside bumps, hills and rises, especially if they're close to the line of your putt.

Putts break toward drain areas
Those tightly mown greenside spots that your ball finds when you short-side the green are always below the level of the putting surface.

Putts break away from bunkers
The last thing a course designer— and especially the superintendent— wants is water draining into a bunker.

Putts break toward the sun
Grass grows all day long, following the path of the sun. When the blades are at their longest, expect serious grain toward the setting sun.

289

WATCH THE WATER
This age-old trick allows you to picture subtle breaks
By Ed Ibarguen

If you consistently have a tough time determining which way putts will break, simply imagine pouring water onto the green near your ball and visualize the direction that the water will run. This will help you with even subtle breaks in the green, because 95 percent of the time, the ball tends to roll in the same direction that water drains off the green.

288

GET AS LOW AS YOU CAN GET
The closer you are to the green's surface, the better your read
By PGA Tour player Camilo Villegas

My green-reading posture isn't for show—it gives me the angle I need to determine slope. I didn't always drop down to the ground like I do now, but I've always tried to get as close to the surface of the green as possible to read putts. Often, I'd step into a greenside bunker to set my eyes near the level of the green. But you don't even have to do that. Most modern courses feature elevated greens, so there's a good chance you can get your eyes close to the putting surface by standing a few yards off the green. Try it a few times and you'll see how easy it is to get a consistent read. It's the same principle as hanging a picture on the wall. You check if you hung it correctly by looking the top edge of the frame and seeing if it's leaning to the left or right, and you hang most frames at eye level.

ULTIMATE GREEN-READING
Mark Sweeney's Zero Line approach is fast becoming the new way to read greens

290

FIND THE ZERO LINE
Simplify your reads by coming to grips with the game's hottest technique
By Mark Sweeney,
AimPoint Technologies

I don't care how crazy a green looks, there are multiple points on its surface from which you can aim dead straight at the hole—a perfect balance between left and right break. And this happens for every possible pin location on every green ever constructed.

Knowing that this left/right balance exists—and then being able to locate its center for the particular putt you're facing—is the secret to demystifying slope and its effect on the ball's roll. It's also the foundation of my green-reading technique based on the information we've gathered by applying AimPoint technology to hundreds of

RULE 1
Putts that start dead on the Zero Line feature a net break of zero—aim at the hole.

RULE 2
Putts originating to the left of the Zero Line break to the right, regardless of whether they're uphill or downhill.

greens on the PGA Tour. Its name? The Zero Line.

The quickest way to come to grasp with the Zero Line is to think of a perfectly flat putting surface with a hole cut in the dead center. Since there isn't any slope to this surface, there are an infinite number of Zero Lines—every putt is a straight putt. Now, imagine lifting the rear of this putting green to create a straight back-to-front

slope. Suddenly, those infinite number of Zero Lines boil down to a single one for each possible hole position: a straight line that runs from the back of the green through the cup and through the front of the green. Any putt off this line will feature some amount of break.

Of course, most greens are tilted like this, but they also feature high points, low points, tiers, etc. Nonetheless, the Zero

RULE 4
Putts to the right of the Zero Line break left, regardless if they're uphill or downhill. Break increases the farther the putt originates from the Zero Line.

RULE 3
The closer the putt originates to the Zero Line, the less amount of break you'll need to calculate. This is true for all putts.

ZERO LINE

Line rule applies, it's just that it becomes more of a curved line instead of straight, but it always runs from near the high point above the hole, across the hole, and to near the lowest point below the hole.

When most golfers start learning about the Zero Line, they often struggle because they try to draw it across the entire green. The secret is that you only need to worry about what the Zero Line

is doing near the cup, say within 20 feet, because your goal isn't to sink more 30-footers. Your goal is to make more of the mid-range and short putts you've been missing due to bad reads. Limiting your comprehension of the Zero

"Any putt off the Zero Line will feature some amount of break."

Line to the area around the hole makes the process simple and infinitely easier to comprehend. Our laser-mapping system can trace the Zero Line across any green in milliseconds. Once you become comfortable with the system, you'll do likewise.

Why does the Zero Line matter, and how exactly does it affect your putt's roll? The above shows you all you need to know.

BUNKER PLAY

You missed on your approach or drive and ended up in the sand. That used to be a big deal, but armed with the following 62 tips you'll escape any bunker on your first swing.

IMPORTANT! The ball goes where the sand goes, not in the direction your clubface is pointing.

291

THE EASY WAY TO DOMINATE FROM SAND

Change your face angle—not your swing—to beat any bunker lie

By Mike Malaska

Simplify your sand woes by taking your normal stance and making your full, regular swing. The only key adjustment is to open your clubface when the ball is sitting up, square it if the ball is partly submerged, and hood it if the ball is buried *[see tips, right]*. Each of these clubface positions allows you to displace varying amounts of sand when your club enters and swings through the bunker. An open face takes less sand; a closed face takes more. All you really need to concern yourself with is hitting behind the ball and taking the right amount of sand for the shot at hand, which you do by changing the position of your clubface (open,

292
BALL UP = OPEN FACE
This allows your wedge to skid more than dig and take minimal sand.

293
BALL DOWN = SQUARE FACE
This allows the leading edge to dig a little deeper and take more sand.

294
BALL BURIED = CLOSED FACE
This allows the toe to really dig into the bunker and displace a lot of sand.

square or closed). It's important to realize that the ball goes where the sand goes, and the sand goes in the direction of your swing, not where your clubface is pointed. Set the face according to the lie and go for it.

HOW TO SET UP FOR SAND SUCCESS

Nailing your address position when you're in a bunker makes easy work of most sandy lies

MATCH YOUR BUNKER STANCE TO YOUR SWING

Allowing for your natural motion is the fast track to blasting out and on

By Kellie Stenzel

When you're in a bunker you don't have to do anything special—you can set up square like you do with a normal lie in the fairway. Golfers who aim to the left of the target in the sand do so because they've opened the clubface and are trying to hit a cut shot. That's usually more trouble than it's worth, but for some players, an open stance beats a square one in sand. Check the guide at right to find out which type of setup works best with your natural swing, then go blast it close.

295

IF YOU'RE A SLOW SWINGER, OR YOU TEND TO SLICE THE BALL...

SET UP SQUARE

Aim your sand wedge at your target, and set your feet parallel left of your target line. When you go to swing, swing along your target line.

WHY IT WORKS

Slicers tend to open the face too much at impact. If you set up with your feet pointed left and the face open to your swing line, you could experience disastrous results. Low swing-speed players need as much power as possible in the sand, and opening the face usually results in a shorter shot.

296

IF YOU SWING FAST, OR YOU TEND TO HOOK THE BALL...

SET UP OPEN

Align your body slightly left of your target and set your clubface square to the target. Your clubface should look open to you.

WHY IT WORKS

Fast swings are power swings, so opening the clubface relative to your stance (and swing) line gives you better distance control and a higher, softer bunker shot. If you hook, setting the face open at address means there's less chance that it will close at impact.

297
DON'T FORGET TO DIG IN
This oft-overlooked step is actually the secret to making sand play easy
By Mark Hackett

Golfers are so concerned with mechanics that they often overlook the art of "digging in" and wonder why they have difficulty blasting out.
My simple: As you get into address, really dig in with your feet. Most golfers do a weak version of a shuffle. The more you dig your feet into the sand, the more you lower the bottom of your swing arc below the surface of the bunker. This allows you to enter the sand behind the ball, swing directly underneath the ball, and exit the sand in front of the ball.

299
MAKE YOUR SETUP AN UMBRELLA
This practice routine makes you a sand expert in no time
By Laird Small

STEP 1
Draw a line in the sand that arcs around your body. Think of this line as an umbrella. Draw a second line from the center of the umbrella—this is the umbrella's handle. Position the ball on the handle line and take your stance [photo, above].

STEP 2
Swing your arms along the umbrella line. You'll notice that as your arms swing in the direction of the arc on the way back to the ball, they pull your sternum over the handle of the umbrella. This forward body move allows you to enter the sand closer to the ball and exit the sand in front of the ball, taking the perfect-size divot.

298
PICTURE TAKING THE PERFECT DIVOT
Make it Danish-sized for foolproof escapes
By Steve Bosdosh

Spend 15 minutes in a practice bunker the next time you visit the range. Without hitting any balls, picture a cheese Danish lying in the sand between the center of your stance and your left heel. The filling in the Danish represents the ball. All you have to do is sweep the entire danish out of the sand. If your divot is larger than a Danish, you hit the shot fat. To fix that, use less wrist cock and more body turn so your swing flattens out through impact. If the divot is smaller than a Danish, you hit it thin, so focus more intently on creating that Danish-sized divot. Once you make the Danish on five consecutive swings, drop a ball down and repeat the same swing.

ESCAPING THE SAND ON YOUR FIRST SWING

These proven bunker moves are all you need to perfect your escape technique

300

Rod Lidenberg says
PRACTICE SWINGING UNDER THE BALL

Think of your ball in the bunker as a three-layer cake: The ball is the first layer, the sand is the second layer and the base of the bunker is the third. The trick is to cut the second layer out without touching the other two. A good way to practice this is to place a ball on a tee, as high as if you were going to hit driver. Make your regular bunker swing and try to hit the tee away so the ball just drops at your feet. This forces you to **keep the club level to the ground on both sides of the ball,** good advice for taking the right-sized divot.

301

Robert Baker says
KICK YOUR KNEES TOWARD THE TARGET

Your hands hold the club, but your shoulders are what power it through the sand. Turn your front shoulder left of the target through impact. Most players simply lift their left shoulder—a move that buries the club too deep into the sand. Also, from the top of your backswing, kick both knees toward the target. **This move effectively shortens the right side of your body, giving you a sweeping upswing through the sand.**

302

Brady Riggs says
REMEMBER YOUR 4 KEYS

Make the following adjustments for easier escapes:
1) Make sure to turn through the shot like you would with an iron in the fairway.
2) Pull your feet in closer together. This will help you produce a faster swing and power more sand—and the ball—toward the target.
3) Keep moving your body, arms and club into a full finish.
4) You don't have a solid stance in sand, so keep your feet grounded as best you can.

303
Steve Bosdosh says
SWING LIKE YOU'RE SKIPPING ROCKS

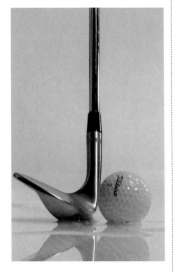

304
Todd Sones says
MAKE A "T" WHEN YOU SET UP

305
Shawn Humphries says
CHIP IT INSTEAD OF BLASTING IT

The next time you're in a bunker, imagine you're standing in a pool of shallow water. Now, instead of thinking about burying your wedge into the sand and exploding the ball out, imagine you're smoothly skipping the sole of your wedge off the water. **This skipping image gives you the proper feel of gliding your sand wedge under the ball**—just like skipping a flat rock off water. This image will help you take a shallow, splashing divot that will carry your ball onto the green.

At address, make sure your shoulder line and shaft line form a "T." **Your job is to maintain the "T" by swinging the club with your arms and your wrists, using minimum shoulder movement.** Keep your chest pointed down and swing your arms and hands underneath your body. This lets the club enter the sand with the loft you established at address. Move to your left side through impact and watch the ball fly high and land like a butterfly with sore feet.

Instead of hitting a long bunker blast (one of the toughest shots you can try), chip the ball out of the bunker. **A chip is easier to hit and easier to control once it lands on the green,** and you don't have to worry about making a big swing and taking the right amount of sand. Use your regular chipping technique and make a crisp pop on the ball. Try to catch the ball before the sand. You'll need more swing speed than for a normal chip, because the sand will slow the club down and you need to roll it 40-50 feet.

THINK YOUR WAY TO BETTER SAND SHOTS

It's often what you do before you take your stance and make your swing that makes the difference

HOW TO PLAN A GREAT ESCAPE

Use these keys to keep from turning a little trouble into big trouble

By Laird Small

The ultimate bunker shot: Short and right on No. 7 at Pebble Beach, with about 60 feet to the pin. While you may have only seen this scenario on TV, what you need to escape this situation is the same thing you use to get the ball out of any other greenside-bunker lie: a plan of attack. Here's how to make one.

306
LOOK AROUND

Designate "can't miss" areas. In this situation there's no bailout area. Fly the green and you're in the Pacific; roll it off and you're in the back bunker. Look for these score-wrecking spots before taking your address and then play away from them.

307
CHECK THE GREEN

This back-to-front sloping green is receptive to the shot I'm playing, but the story would be completely different from the back bunker. Check the slope just like you would on a putt to make sure you land the ball in the right spot.

308
PICK YOUR SPOT

This is a difficult shot, so your first priority is getting out and on the green. And since the only trouble is long, aim to land your ball between the apron and the pin. If you get greedy and go for the flag, there's a good chance you'll hit the ball too far.

309
CHECK THE LIP

Your options from a shallow bunker are a lot more plentiful than when you have to carry a big lip. In the latter, opt for a more lofted club than one you know will give you the distance you need. You don't want to carom off the lip and back into the bunker.

313

PICK THE RIGHT CLUB IN SAND
Simple math helps you dial in any distance from the bunker
By John Elliott, Jr.

Some bunkers feature heavy sand, while others are filled with fluffy sand. Sometimes there's a lot of it, and other times you feel like you're playing off hardpan. This makes it difficult to determine how far a bunker shot will fly. In the end, however, your goal is to get on the green. If you get close, great. This actually takes pressure off your short game—you don't need to be ultra-exact with your distances. As a rule, a swing from a bunker will fly the ball roughly half as far as the same swing with the same club in the fairway *[see chart, below]*. Another rule to follow: don't fall in love with your sand wedge. Your other wedges, even your 9-iron, can work wonders.

310

SET YOUR BASE
Take a wider stance and play the ball in the middle or even slightly back of middle in your stance. Place about 60 percent of your weight on your left leg for this shot, to make sure you don't enter the sand too soon.

311

KEEP THE FACE SQUARE
There's more than enough loft built into your sand wedge, so don't open it up. Also, make sure you break your wrists on your backswing—this'll help you produce speed and hit the sand first. If you try to sweep the ball out, you'll catch it thin.

312

PICK THE RIGHT CLUB
A good rule of thumb is that your full greenside bunker swing (hands to 10 o'clock in your backswing and 2 o'clock in your follow-through) goes a third the distance of the club's normal carry. If you can't reach your target, drop down to a pitching wedge.

FULL-SWING DISTANCES		
CLUB	*IN FAIRWAY*	*IN SAND*
LW	70 yds	35 yds
SW	85 yds	40 yds
GW	100 yds	50 yds
PW	115 yds	55 yds
9-iron	130 yds	65 yds
8-iron	145 yds	75 yds

HOW TO BEAT BUNKER SLOPES
Use these step-by-step procedures to handle two common bunker lies

BLAST FROM AN UPSLOPE
Lean back and let 'er rip
By Mike LaBauve

Your ball is on the upslope of a bunker. If the pin is close, this lie is an advantage—the ball will fly extra high and land quickly. But if you're hitting to a far pin or into the wind, it becomes much more difficult. The key to this shot is to get your body on the same angle as the incline of the bunker by aligning your shoulders with the slope.

314

SELECT THE RIGHT CLUB
Use your 56-degree wedge—the slope will add loft. A 60-degree wedge will send the ball straight up, and you might leave it in the bunker. Take a wider-than-normal stance and dig your downhill foot in.

315

TILT YOUR SHOULDERS
You should feel like your shoulders are tilted with the hill. That's good, because you need to swing up the slope. Make a few practice swings above the ball, getting a feel for moving the clubhead on the same angle as the hill you're standing on.

316

HANG BACK
Because the ball will hit the green and stop with little roll, take a full swing and try to fly the ball all the way to the hole. The slope will want to stop your swing at impact, so try to hang back on your right side a little longer so your wedge glides through unimpeded.

BLAST FROM A DOWNSLOPE
Think "high to low" for a great escape
By Mike LaBauve

Your ball has come to rest on a downslope in the bunker. The smart play here is to make a "high-to-low" bunker swing (i.e., one that starts at a high position in your backswing and finishes much lower than normal). Follow the steps below.

317

MATCH THE SLOPE
Tilt your shoulders and hips to match the slope. If you do it correctly, your left shoulder will sit below your right shoulder the same amount that your left foot sits below your right foot. Dig your left foot deeper into the sand than your right for extra support.

318

SWING DOWN
If you make your normal swing here, your club will hit too far behind the ball, skip off the sand and strike the ball on its equator. Swing down the slope. Take a few practice swings over the ball to ingrain the feel of moving the club from high to low.

319

KEEP YOUR HANDS LOW
Enter the sand about an inch behind the ball. Once your club makes contact with the sand, keep your hands low to the ground all the way into your follow-through. Fight the pull of gravity—it's okay to hang back on your right side on this one.

THE BUNKER-SHOT GRID:

21 WAYS TO BEAT TRICK LIES IN SAND
Expert advice to adapt your technique for the shot at hand

	Top 100 Teacher **DAVID GLENZ**	Top 100 Teacher **ROD LIDENBERG**	Top 100 Teacher **SCOTT SACKETT**
STEP 1	**320 YOUR BASIC BUNKER SHOT** Set up to the ball with the clubface slightly open and with your toe line pointing 10 feet left of your target. Dig your feet into the sand and aim a few feet left of the hole. Don't overdo it—most players cut across the ball too much on bunker shots, and aiming too far left will exacerbate this problem.	**323 PUNCH FROM A FAIRWAY BUNKER** If the front of the green is clear of obstacles, grab a 6-, 7- or 8-iron, depending on your distance to the pin, and plan a hard punch shot. 	**326 SAND LOB SHOT** Use your lob wedge instead of your sand wedge. Take your normal sand setup, playing the ball slightly forward of your stance, and open the face a few degrees.
STEP 2	**321 Make a 75% backswing with normal rotation,** then try to enter the sand two or three inches behind the ball and leave a dollar-bill-sized divot. Make an aggressive move with a full follow-through.	**324** Set up with the ball back of center and the shaft leaning forward. Align the clubface square to the target. Start your swing by hinging your wrists quickly back in a narrow arc. **Cut your backswing when your hands reach hip height—that's all the power you'll need.**	**327 Spread your feet so that they're outside your shoulders and buckle your knees inward.** Kink in your right knee a little more than your left, so that your body tilts at a small angle.
STEP 3	**322** To reach a pin on the other side of the green, take a shallower divot (like you're skimming the surface). **If the pin is close, shorten your swing and take a bit more sand.**	**325** From the top, pinch your knees and focus on making ball-first contact. **Keep your wrists firm at impact**—you don't want to lose the clubshaft angle you created at address.	**328** Make your everyday swing. **Lowering your stance lowers the bottom of your swing arc, so you displace more sand underneath the ball.** That mass of sand pushes the ball up more than it does out. Give it a good swing—you'll need some extra gas to carry the ball the distance you need.

Top 100 Teacher	Top 100 Teacher	Top 100 Teacher	Top 100 Teacher
DONALD CRAWLEY	**EDEN FOSTER**	**SCOTT SACKETT**	**BILL FORREST**

329 BLAST IT DEEP WITH A HYBRID
Use your iron swing with a hybrid club and you can still clear the front lip of the bunker and move the ball down the fairway or maybe even reach the green. (If you don't have a hybrid in your bag, get one!)

332 BUST IT FROM A BURIED LIE
Realistically, you can't do much more to the ball than dislodge it. But guess what? That's all you have to do!

335 HIGH-SPIN SAND SHOT
Use your normal setup and swing, but instead of making a full follow-through and turning all the way through to the target, lift the club out of the sand quickly by bending your left elbow after impact.

338 THE BODY-WEIGHT ESCAPE
Regardless of any move you make in your bunker swing, you must start with your weight left, and rotate more weight to the left. When you swing like this your club automatically bottoms out in the center of your stance.

330 Aim slightly left of your target because this shot will drift a little to the right. **Set up with your weight balanced evenly between your feet** and play the ball off your left cheek.

333 Dig your back foot deeper in the sand than your front. **Use whichever of your wedges has the most bounce.**

336 It should feel like you're trying to get the **shaft straight up and down** as soon as you make contact with the sand.

339 **Start with about 55 percent of your weight on your left side.** As you swing the club back, keep that weight over your left side. No shifting or swaying!

331 Don't try to sweep the club back like a wood—make an upright backswing like you would

with a 7-iron, then bring the club down on the back of the ball, **squeezing it against the sand.**

334 Make your normal sand swing than pound that stupid bunker. **Literally bury your clubhead in the sand.** Don't expect any follow-through, just a soft rebound effect as your club emerges lazily from the sand and the ball sails up and onto the green.

337 The thing to remember is that **you want a more vertical exit angle when you need extra spin to stop the ball close to the hole,** and a shallow exit angle when you don't want spin.

340 Through impact, rotate even more of your weight to the left side. At the end of your swing, all of your weight should be on your left side.

BUNKER SHOT TOP SECRETS
Inside info that turns sand shots into works of art

341

KEEP THE CLUBFACE OPEN
Stop-action photos prove it's the best way to make a great escape
By Mike LaBauve

Your goal for most bunker shots is to keep the face from shutting down, which allows the sole of the club and the bounce angle to help your wedge glide through the sand and not dig in too deeply.

Notice in the bottom sequence of photos how the face of the sand wedge stays open all the way through the sand. You can grill pancakes on this clubface and not spill an ounce of batter! In the top

WRONG

1 The clubface is turning only a little at this point, but it's turning nonetheless.

2 You can see the underside of the club—evidence that the face is rotating. You're really losing loft.

3 The ball isn't riding on a cushion of sand, it's riding *in* a cushion of sand. The benefits of the loft are officially lost.

RIGHT

1 The club exits the bunker with the same amount of loft it started with at address.

2 When you use your wedge correctly, it creates a cushion of sand that propels the ball up and out.

3 Even this deep into the swing, the face is flat—zero hand manipulation. The ball is up and on its way.

sequence, the face is rotating—you can see how much less loft there is on the club as it moves through the sand. This type of clubface rotation is good for full swings from the fairway and tee box, but not in the sand.

4 This is a great clubhead position for a full swing, where you want to release the club, but this ball is coming up short.

4 If you can hold the face steady through impact like this, you'll get the ball out every time.

HOW TO HANDLE DIFFERENT TYPES OF SAND
Use your feet to determine the type of sand, and adjust accordingly
By Dom DiJulia

Do your feet sink into the sand when you walk in the bunker? Or do you feel like you're walking on top of the sand, and the ball is sitting on top of it as well? Knowing the difference is important, because if you use your regular bunker swing in fluffy sand, the ball will go nowhere. Here's how to adjust your swing to match the sand conditions you determine in your pre-shot routine.

342 IF THE SAND IS FLUFFY...

Your club will stick in fluffy sand, so hitting a good explosion means taking a very large divot with a very fast swing. Swing three-quarters back and make a complete follow-through.

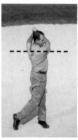

343 IF THE SAND IS THIN...

There's less sand for your club to extract so the ball will come out "hotter" than normal. Swing from hip-high back to hip-high in your finish. This will give you 10 yards in the air.

SIX TOP 100 TEACHERS ON:

ADJUSTING FOR UNIQUE CONDITIONS
Vary your arsenal to easily handle whatever the course chooses to throw at you

344

Brady Riggs says
DIG YOUR WAY OUT OF NASTY BUNKERS

From a poorly maintained bunker, lean your weight toward your left side to create a digging angle of attack, and set the face square. **The feeling you're after is one of carving the ball out with the leading edge,** not splashing it out with the sole. Hit just behind the ball and drive the leading edge down into the sand (but don't drive the clubhead so deep that you leave it in the bunker). It should feel like you're chunking a pitch shot from the fairway.

345

Mike Adams says
STEP OUT WHEN THE BALL IS BACK

On this lie, don't be afraid to move your right foot up and out of the sand and place it on the hill behind the bunker. You might think this stance is just as limiting as the one with your feet close together, but **it actually turns this tough lie into a regular downhill bunker blast.** For that shot, the key is to adjust your body so that your swing is level with the slope.

346

Steve Bosdosh says
GET STEEP WITH A BALL BELOW YOUR FEET

For this shot you'll need extra bend in your knees at address in order to get your club down to the ball. More important, they'll have to remain bent during your swing or you'll catch the top half of the ball. Control your knees and this becomes a relatively simple bunker shot. **Try to keep your spine flat— this automatically creates a steep swing—and take the club back and through normally,** remembering to keep your knees flexed.

347

Ed Ibarguen says
GO SLOW TO FAST IF THE SAND IS WET

You don't want to start off fast and long and then slow down in a wet bunker. That leads to deceleration. Make a shorter backswing, stopping your hands between halfway to three-quarters back. On your downswing, **Smoothly speed up so that the fastest part of your swing occurs as your club is digging through the sand.** Use your body—turn your chest and hips toward the target as you power your wedge through impact.

348

Dom DiJulia says
FLIP YOUR HANDS TO CARRY HIGH LIPS

Use your lob wedge and set up square to your target. Play the ball almost off your left heel, and tilt your upper body away from the target. Aim for a spot an inch behind the ball, and as you enter the sand, keep your weight back and allow the club to pass your hands. **It should feel like you're slapping the bottom of the club against the sand under the ball,** and your right hand should flip under your left hand so that the face points straight up in your follow-through.

349

Jason Carbone says
POUND SAND TO BUST ONE FROM THE LIP

Your ball has plugged in a sand bunker a foot or so below the lip. Lower your right shoulder to get your shoulders more even with the slope. Then **take the club back on a steep, V-shaped path** and bring it down hard into the sand just below the ball, driving the heel of the club into the hill. There's no need to make a conscious follow-through—the concussion of the club hitting the sand will drive the ball up and out of the bunker.

WHEN ALL ELSE FAILS...

Turn to these new bunker-escape methods and get the ball up and out in one swing

350

TRY THE CAN'T-MISS BLAST SWING

It's different, but this new method works—even for the most inept bunker players

By Bruce Patterson

Whether you're aware of it or not, you're struggling in sand because you're not effectively using the bounce of your club. You're either digging the club into the bunker or so afraid of digging that you fail to take any sand at all. Start with a new grip. Rotate your hands to the left on the handle to the

weakest position you can muster. You might feel uncomfortable with this ultra-weak hold, but don't be too concerned. Position the ball a few inches behind the center of your stance—again, trust me here—and make your normal swing, passing the clubhead firmly through the sand just behind

the ball. As you swing through impact you'll feel the clubface slide open as it contacts the sand, which is what you want and why you took such a weakened grip. This opening action activates the bounce of your club, helping it glide instead of dig. I've seen this method work for just about everyone who's tried it.

TAKEAWAY
Your right arm will be above your left due to the ultra-weak hold. Don't worry about it.

LEFT-HAND GRIP
Make it as weak as possible.

RIGHT-HAND GRIP
Should be ultra-weak to help the face open through impact and activate the bounce on your wedge.

352

HIT THE SIT-DOWN BUNKER SHOT
It proves just how easy bunker play can be
By John Elliott, Jr.

Try hitting bunker shots while sitting down. Find a flat portion of the bunker, plop down in the sand, cross your legs and...just kidding. There isn't any benefit to practicing sand shots from your rear end. The only lesson is that, yes, it can be done, and fairly easily. I use this trick to start many of my short-game schools, if only to demonstrate how easy bunker play can be. It's not the mysterious voodoo you probably think it is. It's really as simple as "hit the sand and let the sand carry the ball out of the bunker." Once you get it into your mind that sand shots aren't as difficult as they appear (or as you make them out to be), you'll have an extra bit of confidence.

351

LET GO WITH YOUR RIGHT HAND
The last-ditch way to try to blast it on and close
By Shawn Humphries

The easiest way to hit a soft bunker shot is to slow the club down just as it reaches impact. Unfortunately a lot of you probably do this already by either decelerating or simply sticking the clubhead deep into the sand. Both methods typically leave the ball in the bunker. Instead you should use my one-hand technique, in which you allow your right hand to come off the club as you pass through the impact zone.

1. Take your normal setup with your weight slightly left, the face a bit open and the ball up in your stance.

2. Make your normal swing, but let go of the grip with your right hand just as the clubhead makes contact with the sand.

3. Finish the shot with your left hand only. Don't stop your swing just because you've let go with your right hand. The ball should come out soft and stop quickly.

TROUBLE SHOTS

You're going to miss on your drives and approach shots from time to time. Here are our top teachers' 53 best ways to get back in the hole and card par at the worst.

353

TEST THE TROUBLE FIRST
Your practice swing is the key to easy escapes
By John Elliott, Jr.

Any time you're in a situation with an unusual or tough lie like thick rough, sand, leaves, concrete, etc., you must take several practice swings to feel how the club and your swing will be affected by the conditions. For example, if your ball is resting on a walkway or road, you'll find that the club accelerates and bounces through impact. But when you're hitting out of rough, the club will slow down and twist, while in a pile of dead leaves it might simply bury. The key is to test the conditions with your practice swing in the same environment as your real lie. Notice that I've swung through a similar pile of leaves during my practice attempt, not from the fairway or next to the cart. This gives me the right feel for the shot. After you've actually attempted to hit the ball, make a mental note of how the ball reacted for future reference.

TRIAL RUN
Take a practice swing from a lie that's similar to the trouble you're in to get a feel for the shot.

354

HOW TO AVOID TROUBLE FROM THE START

Look for miss spots then before you pull the trigger

By Rick Grayson

The tee box on a drivable par 4 is a good place to learn how to minimize your chances of finding trouble, even if you make a good swing. Sure, the green is in range, but are the potential trouble situations worth the risk in the event you make a mistake? Run through this checklist to make sure you're not unwittingly placing yourself in danger and risking a "blow-up" score.

356

GO FOR IT IF...

[√] You're confident you can carry all hazards off the tee.

[√] There's a breeze at your back—10 mph of wind equals as much as 20 extra yards.

[√] You can land your drive within this 30-yard slot.

355

DON'T GO IF...

[X] You're a strong wedge player. Lay up, wedge it on, and you can still make birdie.

[X] You've missed more than half your fairways up to this point.

[X] You fight a slice, and there's big trouble right.

TROUBLE SHOT BASICS
Start here when mapping a strategy for getting back in the fairway or getting on the green

TAKE A CONSERVATIVE APPROACH
Getting back to the short grass is your smartest play more often than not
By Steve Bosdosh

358
HINGE QUICKLY
On your backswing, hinge the club back quickly so that your wrists are fully cocked by the time your hands reach your thighs.

Your lie in the rough is thick, covering the ball on all sides. Accept that you're not going to hit the green. This is gouge time—a 9-iron at best. You're going to use a lot of the elements from your bunker swing, but instead of sliding your club through sand, you'll slam it steeply into the back of the ball.

357
HUG THE BALL
Stand closer to the ball and choke up so the shaft is more upright than usual for the club you've chosen. Aim slightly right of your landing area and play the ball back of center. Also, increase your grip pressure—otherwise, the grass will turn the clubface over and the ball will go left. Forward-press your hands so the shaft leans toward the target.

359
PULL DOWN
Swing down sharply with extra force. Feel like you're pulling the handle of the club down into the ball. Keep your legs quiet (notice how little they move in these photos).

LET THE LIE BE YOUR GUIDE
Assess the situation, then change your swing to match the lie
By Eden Foster

362
SWING STEEP FROM ROUGH
This quick setup trick automatically gives you a grass-busting swing
By Jason Carbone

When the deep grass is growing opposite the direction of your target, it's going to slow down the clubhead, grab the hosel and shut the clubface. Sounds tricky, but executing this shot and getting the ball on the green is 90 percent setup. Take an extra club (you'd take less club if the grass was growing toward the target), stand a little closer to the ball and play it slightly back of its normal position. Standing closer will help you swing the club more up-and-down and reduce the time it spends in contact with the grass. Open the clubface a few degrees to offset the shutdown effect of the grass and grip the club tighter. If your normal grip pressure is a 4 on a 1-to-10 scale, make this one a 6.5.

363
MAKE BAD LIES LOOK GOOD
A little house cleaning goes a long way
By John Elliott. Jr.

Don't let lies fool you— you're not always stuck with the one you see when you first arrive at your ball. Spend a few moments picking up the leaves, sticks, etc., around your lie. After removing the debris, you'll discover that your ball isn't sitting so badly. As you can see from the photos below, this bad lie is actually pretty good when you eliminate the rubbish.

360
HIT A LAYUP
The ball is too deep in the rough to get the solid contact you need to travel the full distance to the green. Take your 5-hybrid or 6-iron and swing down sharply on the ball, almost like a punch shot. Since all you're worried about here is clean contact, your finish will be short (hands even with your shoulders).
THE RULE:
Ball sitting low, finish low.

361
GO FOR IT
Once you make the decision to knock this ball on, don't hold back. However, this doesn't mean you should swing out of your socks. Firm up your grip pressure (an "8" on a 1 to 10 scale) and smoothly swing to a full finish with a full release of the clubhead. This means that your finish will be high (hands way above your shoulders).
THE RULE:
Ball sitting high, finish high.

SIX TOP 100 TEACHERS ON:

HANDLING DIFFICULT LIES
How to deal with slope and obstacles when going for the green

| 364 | 365 | 366 |

Peter Krause on
**BLASTING A BALL
BELOW YOUR FEET**

Donald Crawley on
**SWEEPING THE BALL
OFF A DOWNHILL LIE**

Mike Lopuszynski on
**HITTING STRAIGHT
FROM A SIDEHILL**

Take a more stable stance and swing with your hands and arms to make easy work of this seemingly difficult lie. Widen your stance and flare both feet out about 45 degrees (point your knees outward too). It should feel like you're riding a horse. These adjustments will stabilize your lower body. Then **squat your upper body down to the ball and make a swing using only your hands and arms.** You'll want to aim right of the target because an armsy swing like this will close the clubface early.

If the slope you're on isn't too severe (let's say your left foot is only a few inches below your right), you only need to fine-tune your setup and swing. First, set your body, including your shoulders, parallel with the slope. Take the club back along the slope. Since the ground behind the ball is higher than the ground in front of it, your backswing will be much steeper. Fight the urge to strand weight on your left foot. **Swing down the slope while turning your hips** so that they're open to the target at impact.

Your goal from this lie is to maintain your posture. If you straighten up, you'll hit a low screamer off to the right. Swing at 70 percent so you can keep your balance. You'll need every inch of your club to get down to the ball, so **make sure you're holding it at the very end of the handle—or use a longer club with a shorter swing.**

367

Bryan Gathright on
BEATING A BALL ABOVE YOUR FEET

Long iron

Short iron

A lie with the ball above your feet will cause your ball to curve to the left. But the amount of curve depends on the club in your hands. Because they have more loft and a more upright lie, **short irons are more affected by slope than long irons.** Because of this difference, you don't need to aim so far to the right when you're swinging your mid to long irons from this lie. Aim the center of your clubface at your target first. If you're hitting a short iron, aim your shoulders, hips and feet 10 yards to the right.

368

Anne Cain on
PUNCHING A RESTRICTED SWING

M ost golfers try to swing slow here, but that leads to mis-hits. Keep your speed the same, but make a smaller swing so you can **pull the club back after impact.** Take the club back by hinging your wrists quickly and fully. Swing your hands back only to hip height. Then, power the club down with your arms sharply on the ball—try and take a steep divot. As soon as you make contact, pull the club away from your target, almost as if it's rebounding off the ball.

369

Bill Forrest
BATTING A BALL OFF A SEVERE SLOPE

T he secret to this lie is to remain standing tall. You can take a full hack if you need to, but the harder you swing, the greater the chances are that you'll lean into the hill to maintain your balance. That's when you catch the ball fat. **Try to finish your swing standing as tall as you did at address.** To ensure that your swing stays sufficiently flat, think about swinging your right arm across your chest after impact.

MIRACLE SAVES

Put these two jaw-dropping escapes in your shot arsenal to save your scores and look cool doing it

THE LEFTY PUNCH

Take a swing from the other side when you can't take your normal stance

By Steve Bosdosh

Your ball is against the base of a tree and you can't stand to the left of the ball. So what? With the club turned upside-down, make a little punch swing from a left-handed stance using a left-handed grip.

371

MAKE A PUTTING STROKE
Since bad things happen when you try to hit this shot too hard, swing the club like it's your putter. Before you hit this shot, make a few practice swings from a similar lie nearby. Find a leaf and try to catch it on the fat part of the toe section.

370

SET UP LEFTY
Stand to the ball in a lefty address position. Rotate your sand wedge so that it points at your target with the toe section hanging down. Set the toe (the fattest portion of the clubhead) directly behind the ball—that's your strike area. Then grip the club left-hand-low, with your right hand at the top of the handle, and position the ball off your left foot.

372 **AVOID WRIST ACTION**
The last thing you want to do with this shot is use a lot of wrist action. That increases your chances of bottoming out too early or too late. Lock your wrists and make a smooth, left-handed putting stroke.

THE BANK-SHOT CHIP
Save par when you don't have enough green to land even a flop shot

By Shawn Humphries

This is a hard chip shot hit into the bank of the hill. The ball shoots straight up after it strikes the hill and lands like a butterfly with sore feet on the green. Use it when you've missed a crowned green to the left or right and settled into a collection area. There's a slope in front of you and, worse yet, very little green between the fringe and the pin. There's not even enough green to hold a high-lofted shot.

373
PICK YOUR TARGET
Find your target on the bank. Generally, it will be a spot about three-quarters up the bank. (Make sure the bank is steep enough so that the force of the ball will cause it to bounce up and not skip forward.)

374
USE YOUR CHIP SETUP
Set up to the ball like you would for a chip shot with your feet close together, your hands pressed forward and your weight favoring the left. The ball should be just a shade back of center in your stance, since the last thing you want to do here is hit up on the ball (you'll add loft and miss the bank completely).

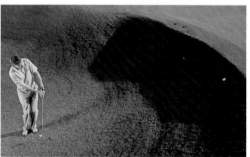

375
GET AGGRESSIVE
Make an extremely aggressive chip shot without any release and with a limited follow-through. Notice how my hands are still in line with the club and how the club hasn't released.

SAVE PAR FROM TRICKY CONDITIONS
How to not let the ground beneath your feet fool you

	Top 100 Teacher **DONALD CRAWLEY**	Top 100 Teacher **DR. GARY WIREN**	Top 100 Teacher **JASON CARBONE**
STEP 1	**376 HIT FROM HARDPAN** Position the ball just forward of the middle of your stance and hover the club above the dirt. Set your weight so that it slightly favors your left side. If your weight is too far forward, you'll swing too steeply. 	**379 HIT FROM A DIVOT** Address the ball as you normally would, then move your feet slightly left so the ball is a bit back in your stance.	**382 HIT FROM WET TURF** Your feet will sink into soggy ground. Offset the fact that your swing arc has been lowered by gripping down on the club a full inch. 
STEP 2	**377** You have plenty of club, **so make a comfortable three-quarter backswing.** If you swing any harder, you'll lose your footing (which isn't that great to begin with since your spikes can't dig into hardpan).	**380** L**ean your entire body toward the target** so that your chest and zipper are ahead of the ball. 	**383** Stand taller to the ball (don't bend as much from your hips) so that you can comfortably hover the club and **line up the leading edge with the ball's equator.** 
STEP 3	**378** Your goal is to **strike the ball and the hardpan at the same time.** Notice how my shoulders, hips and knees are all rotating. Turning like this guarantees you won't come down too steeply and bounce the club off the ground.	**381** Make your normal swing. Steps 1 and 2 ensure that you'll create a more descending blow, which should shoot the ball out of the divot quite easily. Note that **the ball will fly lower and "hotter" out of a divot,** so be careful when choosing where you want to land your shot.	**384** Aim for a spot one inch in front of the ball. Your goal is to **hit the back of the ball and then drive your club into the ground at that spot.** This gives you ball-first contact and negates any interference from the wet turf. A good swing thought is to picture your clubhead and right knee reaching the ball at the same time.

385

HOW TO HANDLE FESCUE
This club-grabbing grass requires extra-special attention
By Eden Foster

The major problem with fescue or any kind of long rough is that it gets between your ball and the clubface. You'll always suffer a loss of distance as a result. Plus, the long grass tends to grab the hosel and close the face, making it impossible to control the ball. A steep cut swing solves both of these problems. With your club approaching the ball on a steeper angle of attack, there's less contact time between the clubface and the grass, so your shots will fly nearly full distance. And since your clubface is open (a natural by-product of a cut path), the shutdown will make everything flush at contact.

HOW TO HIT THIS SHOT
1) Take the club up vertically so that your hands are way above your shoulders.
2) From the top, come down steeply and allow your clubhead to move outside your hands.
3) Swing to the left of the target to complete the over-the-top move and escape the rough with power.

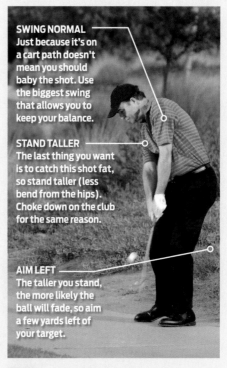

SWING NORMAL
Just because it's on a cart path doesn't mean you should baby the shot. Use the biggest swing that allows you to keep your balance.

STAND TALLER
The last thing you want is to catch this shot fat, so stand taller (less bend from the hips). Choke down on the club for the same reason.

AIM LEFT
The taller you stand, the more likely the ball will fade, so aim a few yards left of your target.

386

HOW TO HIT OFF A CART PATH
Give it a ride from the most unusual lie
By Roger Gunn

Most trouble shots call for "ball-first" contact. You're thinking, "duh." Yes, your club should strike the ball before it contacts the turf on most shots (you don't in sand), but in the ball-first scenarios, it's critical that it happen in that order. If not, you've got a disaster on your hands, and the cart-path lie is no exception. Make a few practice swings in nearby grass with the goal of just nipping the tops of the blades. Once you get a feel for the swing, address the ball on the path and copy the moves at right.

THE TWO BEST SHORT-GAME PLAYS
Learn to drive it low or fly it high to get around any object between you and your target

HIT A SCORING PUNCH
This shot keeps the ball low and moving up the fairway
By Brady Riggs

Your shot has landed in the rough below tree limbs. You need to get the ball back in play by scooting it up the fairway. In the past these situations have led to big numbers that have blown up your entire round. You need a low shot that flies under the obstacle and gets you back into play.

387
WEIGHT LEFT
Set the majority of your weight on your front foot with your hands slightly forward of center, so that the shaft leans toward the target. Visualize a shot that flies low and hard before you take your backswing, which should be shorter than normal.

388
DON'T HANG BACK
On your downswing, shift your weight even more toward the target—don't hang back! The shaft should continue to lean toward the target to both remove loft and help the clubhead work down and through the thick grass.

389
FINISH LOW
Think about getting your chest over your front foot in your follow-through, and cut your swing off when your hands reach chest height. The clubhead should finish at or below the height of your hands with the toe pointing straight at the target.

HOW TO FLY TALL OBSTACLES
Tree trouble? No trouble!
By Brian Mogg

Your drive missed the fairway. Your lie is good—the only trouble is a sizable tree standing between you and the pin. You could make the safe play and hit a half-wedge back to the fairway, but in this situation you need to make something happen in your round. With a few minor adjustments to your setup and swing you should be able to loft the ball high enough to clear the tree and land on the green.

390
OPEN UP
Position the ball forward in your stance, toward your left heel. After soling your club, set your hands even with the ball (don't lean the shaft forward). Also, rotate the clubface open a few degrees (clockwise) to give the club extra loft.

391
GET STEEP
The secret to hitting high shots is steepness—a more vertical downswing where you really hit down on the ball will cause it to rise quickly and fly extra-high. Do this by hinging your wrists aggressively and early in your backswing.

392
FINISH HIGH
Feel like your left ear is behind the ball as you swing through impact, and keep your hands even with or slightly behind the clubhead when you make contact. Follow through as high as possible with your hands finishing higher than your left ear. Now, go make that birdie putt!

CONTROL DISTANCE AND TRAJECTORY
You need both when you're playing escape shots into the green

GET HOME FROM ANYWHERE
Simple setup and backswing changes give you the shot shape and distance you need to attack the green from trouble spots
By Dr. Gary Wiren

You've missed the fairway, and though your lie is good and you're within range of the green, a low-hanging branch prevents you from playing a wedge shot.

STEP 1: Stay aggressive. Never let a tree or its limbs come between you and a chance for birdie.
STEP 2: Determine which is the highest-lofted club in your bag

393
TO HIT THE FULL DISTANCE
Take your normal grip on the end of the handle.

394
TO SUBTRACT 10 YARDS
Now choke down to the middle of the grip. This takes ten yards off the shot.

395
TO SUBTRACT 20 YARDS
If you choke all the way down to the bottom, that subtracts ten more yards.

that will keep the ball under the branch.
STEP 3: Mix and match your grip (how much you choke down on the handle) and backswing length to produce the appropriate distance.

396
TO SUBTRACT 40 YARDS
Use your full choke and shorten your backswing by 10 inches (hands shoulder high).

397
TO SUBTRACT 50 YARDS
Use your full choke and shorten your backswing by 20 inches (hands chest high).

398
TO SUBTRACT 60 YARDS
Use your full choke and shorten your backswing another 30 inches (hands at hip height).

GREENSIDE SUPER SAVES

Pull these savvy plays from your bag of tricks when you miss the green on your approach

399

HOW TO BEAT GNARLY GREENSIDE ROUGH
Treat this shot like a bunker blast for a memorable up-and-down
By Tom Stickney

The trick to playing a chip from long grass is to slide the club under the ball, just like you do when you're in a bunker. That's a good way to think about this shot—picture the blades of grass as grains of sand. Also, you want to limit the amount of time the club spends in contact with the rough, so you need a steeper approach than normal (a flatter approach increases clubface/grass contact time). A steeper approach will also add loft to the shot, which you'll need to stop the ball quickly on the green. You can't count on stopping the shot with spin, because you won't get any. Try to keep the clubface pointing at the sky through impact, and let it glide smoothly under the ball.

Make your swing steep on both sides of the ball to chop the ball from rough and onto the green.

400

CHIP FROM DOWNSLOPE
Pull your right foot back to turn a tricky lie into an easy save
By Mike Malaska

Your ball is on a severe downhill lie near the green. Set up with a shoulder-width stance and position the ball just inside your right foot. Tilt your shoulders to the left until they're even with the slope. (You can flare your left foot a little to maintain your balance.) **Now move your right foot behind you** (away from the target line) by about a foot or so. You now have a clear inside-to-out path that the club can follow to the ball.

Putt with the leading edge from this tricky greenside lie.

401

BLADE IT FROM THE FRINGE
Here's one situation where it pays to catch it thin
By Brady Rggs

Your ball is sitting where the rough and the fringe meet. The lack of grass under the ball means you have no cushion, while the heavy grass behind the ball makes solid contact nearly impossible. While the term "bladed wedge" may send shivers down your spine, it's the perfect shot for this lie. Use your pitching wedge, which has the straightest leading edge of all your wedges. Grip it like you would your putter and address the ball like you're setting up for a putt. Align the leading edge with the equator of the ball and make your normal putting stroke. Your goal is to strike the ball on its equator.

402

HIT A POP PUTT FROM THE ROUGH
Use your putter on short delicate chips from the junk
By Martin Hall

Getting a wedge through rough isn't easy, especially when you're facing short distances around the green. The trick is to realize that you only need to pop the ball out of the rough and let the roll do the rest. There are dozens of ways to accomplish this task, but one is easier than all the rest: pop it out with your putter. Your flatstick is the shortest club in your bag, meaning it's the easiest to control. Plus, it gives you the widest strike area—a good asset when you're swinging though long grass.

Step 1	Step 2	Step 3
From a normal putting stance, position the ball outside your right foot. Set your hands in front of your zipper so the shaft leans toward the target.	Smoothly hinge the club up with your wrists without moving your arms. This is all the backswing you need.	Release your wrist hinge and bring the putterhead into the back of the ball on a descending path. The ball should pop up before it moves forward.

THE GREATEST ESCAPE OF ALL

For gamblers only—a risky play to save strokes and turn heads

PUNCH IT OUT FROM YOUR KNEES
It's not a comedy skit, it's a par-saver!
By Jason Carbone

When you can't reach the ball with your normal stance because the ball lies under an obstruction (in this example, a low-hanging tree branch), grab your shortest hybrid or fairway wood, drop to your knees and follow these steps.

403
THE SETUP

Drop down to your knees and spread them as far as you can to establish a solid base (flare both feet out if you can to make your stance even more stable). Grab your shortest fairway wood or hybrid and choke down all the way to the base of the handle. (Don't use an iron—the ultra-flat shaft arrangement makes it easy for the long hosel on an iron to dig into the ground at impact).

As you settle into position, notice how far the clubface points to the left when you sole your club behind the ball (it happens automatically when you make the shaft flatter). It'll look strange, but don't change it. If you keep your hands ahead of the clubhead through impact, the face will square up and the ball

404

THE SWING

Try to make a baseball swing back and through. Obviously, this is an arms-only motion. Make sure to hinge your wrists and swing your left arm across your chest on your backswing, and release the club across your left shoulder. You'll be surprised how much distance you'll generate.

will fly straight. That's the number-one key for this shot.

The big mistake here is allowing the clubhead to drop down, causing you to hit the ground behind the ball. It's difficult to think about swing plane with such an extreme setup, so hover the club above the ball at address. This allows you to make clean contact even if the clubhead drops, and actually keeps tension to a minimum.

405

THE MUSTS

Make sure your hands get to the ball before your clubhead. Otherwise this shot will hook wildly to the left. And while you may think a short iron might be easier to control, its long hosel set so close to the ground increases the chance that you'll dig it into the turf way before the ball.

STRATEGY

Even your best swings won't always produce the results you want. That's when smarts and strategy come into play—the way you plot your course to ensure you're making all the right moves

HOW TO GET OFF TO A HOT START

Whether you hit a warm-up bucket or not, follow these steps to make your first shot a good one

By Brian Mogg

When you can't get to the course early (and even if you do get there early enough to warm up properly), take the time to run through this five-item checklist before you step up to hit your first tee shot. It won't take long, and it can go a long way toward making that first drive a good one.

406
TARGET YOUR FOCUS

Picture landing the ball in a bull's-eye and erase any negative thoughts. Your first tee shot is important: The positive emotions that come with getting off to a good start can send your energy and focus to the level you need to play your best.

407
COUNT YOUR CLUBS

You're only allowed 14 sticks in your bag, and while your buddies might not call a penalty on you, an official certainly will if you're playing in a formal event. Plus, you want to make sure you didn't leave your trusty 7-iron in the backyard.

409
TAKE A BREAK

Lag behind your group as you walk to the first tee, close your eyes and think about the day ahead. Devise a game plan not only for your swing, but for how you'll conduct yourself during your round. Without this kind of mental strategy, you won't find your groove until it's much too late.

410
CHECK YOUR SWING

Before you make your first swing, take your driver to the top of your backswing, stop, and look over your right shoulder to check your position. You may notice that the club is laid off, or that the clubface is wide open. You'll want to know about these things before you tee off so you won't have to search for clues or experiment with dangerous swing changes.

408
GEAR UP

Run through the pockets in your bag. Some necessities you'll need for every round are a glove, plenty of balls and tees, a pencil, coins or markers and your scorecard. During the summer, make sure you're armed with sunblock and lip balm. You don't want to interrupt your focus by frantically searching for any of these items when you need them.

STRATEGY BASICS
Aiming correctly and controlling your ball flight when you need to will never go out of style

GET YOUR ALIGNMENT RIGHT AT THE START
Avoid missing your targets left or right with this four-step routine
By Scott Munroe

You stand behind the ball on the tee box and pick your target, then take your stance just like you're supposed to. So why does the ball land right of your target, and sometimes miss the fairway or green completely? The answer lies in the fact that when you take your stance, you tend to align your body to the target. But since your body sits to the left of your ball-to-target line, aiming your body at the target means you're aiming your clubface to the right. Follow the steps at right to stop wasting strokes due to poor alignment.

411
Stand behind the ball and select your target (the spot where you want the ball to land). Draw a line from your target back to the ball.

412
Take a sizable—yet comfortable—sidestep to your left and pick a new target, parallel to your original target line, and walk down your new line.

413
Set your eyes back on your original target, step forward and place your right foot on your second line and point the face down the first line.

414
Now set your left foot—your eyes should still be on the original target. Your body is now aligned parallel to your clubface—you won't miss this shot right or left.

THE SIMPLE WAY TO SHAPE SHOTS

Working the ball toward your targets—and away from trouble—is easier than you think

By Jason Carbone

Playing shots with a controlled curve to the right or left allows you to attack certain hole positions, fly the ball away from trouble and hold it into the wind (or let it ride the wind for extra distance). Here's an easy way to fade or draw the ball without tinkering with your swing.

DRAW IT!
Keep your hands above the shaft

Make a practice swing and think "high hands, low clubhead." Rehearse this finish position and you'll automatically guide your swing on a more inside-out plane that prompts you to make an aggressive release through impact in order to keep the clubhead below your hands. An inside path and full release of your hands are the telltale traits of a solid draw swing.

416

FADE IT!
Keep your hands and shaft as close to level as possible

Take your normal address position and make a practice swing. Finish with your hands and the shaft nearly level. It helps to think "low hands, high clubhead." Rehearse this finish position and you'll establish a swing that moves a bit across the line through impact, and that gives you the left-to-right cut spin you need to hit a fade.

CREATING A CUSTOM-MADE DRIVE
Expert advice for tee-box strategy and shotmaking

417
Carol Preisinger on
BLASTING THROUGH THE BREEZE

You're on the tee of a long par 4 playing dead into a steady wind. You need a low, boring drive that flies under the wind.
Step 1: Tee the ball lower so the entire ball is on the clubface, and adjust your ball position so that it's just forward of center. Doing this encourages a more level swing arc through impact.
Step 2: Stop your backswing short of parallel by limiting your wrist hinge. This takes some of the loft off the club and further enhances your chances of keeping the shot low. Then, swing down like normal.

418
Steve Bosdosh on
HITTING A POWER FADE

A power fade is ideal on holes that turn hard to the right or when most of the trouble is up the left side. First, pick a spot between the center of the fairway and the left rough— that's the line your shot travels on before it turns right. Then align your stance to this spot, but point the face down the center of the fairway. These adjustments automatically create the left-to-right curve you're planning on.
It helps if you aim for the outside quadrant of the ball. Striking here increases the likelihood that the ball will fade.

419
Ted Sheftic on
RIDING THE WIND FOR MORE YARDS

You're on the tee with a decent wind at your back. The play here is to produce an extra-high drive so the ball can ride the wind. Keep your tee height the same but play the ball an inch forward of normal. Step out a few inches wider with your right foot and tilt your upper body so that your head is over your right kneecap. Make your normal backswing, but as you come back down try to **hang back on your right side a little longer.** Hanging back helps create a higher launch angle.

420

Jim Murphy on
DRAWING THE BALL WITH POWER

421

Mike Perpich on
SIMPLIFYING PAR-3 CLUB SELECTION

422

Dr. David Wright on
DRIVING WITH CONFIDENCE

Stand on the left side of the tee box, look down the fairway and pick a target between the center of the fairway and the right rough. Tee your ball, take your stance and take one final look at your target. It should feel as though you have to swing out to the right to get the ball started on your line. That's the feeling you want for a draw. **Take the clubhead back low to the ground and slightly inside your target line.** Fight the urge to lift your arms and hands. Then, swing down and out to your target.

The key to beating par 3s is to maximize your chances of hitting the green. To do so you need to survey the tee box carefully and then take full advantage of the situation in terms of club, shot selection, and where you tee the ball. Remember that not only are you allowed to stand outside the teeing area, **you can also move back from the tee markers up to two full club lengths.** Measure this space before selecting a club and position the ball to give yourself the most comfortable shot into the green.

Thinking about your swing is fine when you're at the range, but when you're on the course and stepping into a shot, the last thing you want to think about is folding your right elbow, or how to trigger your downswing. Instead, erase all swing thoughts, **visualize your ball flight and choose a point on the horizon where you want the ball to start.** See it fly out on this line and trace the arc and trajectory you pictured in your mind. Be specific with your imagination. Vague visualizations never do the trick.

PRO-STYLE GAME PLANNING
Club selection tips for the tee box and fairway to ensure your best chance at birdie

423

HOW TO BIRDIE SHORT PAR 4s
A savvy tee shot gives you a chance to make 3
By Brady Riggs

A short par 4 provides you with an opportunity for birdie—if you can hit the fairway. The impulse is to think, "If I crush my driver, I can get really close to the green and make 3." The reality is that if you miss the fairway, your 3 could become a 5—or worse.

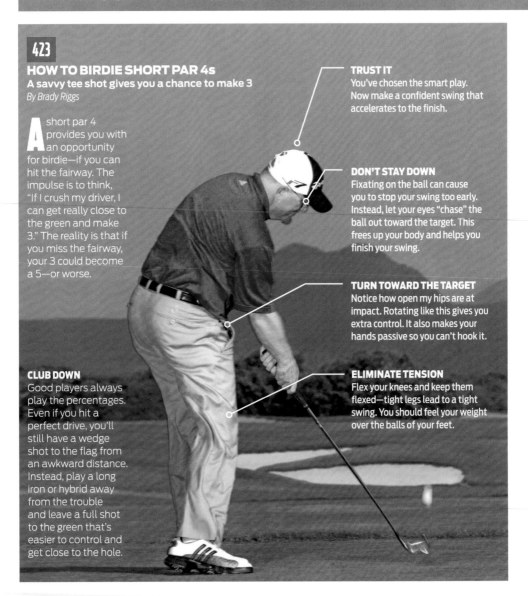

TRUST IT
You've chosen the smart play. Now make a confident swing that accelerates to the finish.

DON'T STAY DOWN
Fixating on the ball can cause you to stop your swing too early. Instead, let your eyes "chase" the ball out toward the target. This frees up your body and helps you finish your swing.

TURN TOWARD THE TARGET
Notice how open my hips are at impact. Rotating like this gives you extra control. It also makes your hands passive so you can't hook it.

ELIMINATE TENSION
Flex your knees and keep them flexed—tight legs lead to a tight swing. You should feel your weight over the balls of your feet.

CLUB DOWN
Good players always play the percentages. Even if you hit a perfect drive, you'll still have a wedge shot to the flag from an awkward distance. Instead, play a long iron or hybrid away from the trouble and leave a full shot to the green that's easier to control and get close to the hole.

HOW TO PLAN A PERFECT APPROACH SHOT
Look for trouble around the green first
By Brady Riggs

Regardless of how good your short game is, every green complex houses trouble spots from which making par is impossible. If you know where these trouble spots are and plan your approach to the green so that if you do miss you won't land in them, you won't be saddled with an automatic bogey. It's the same strategy you use when you're looking for good miss spots from the tee box.

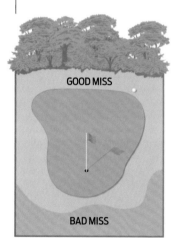

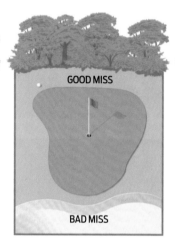

424
IF THE PIN IS UP...
hit the club that will land you in the center of the green.
If your shot flies too far, you'll leave yourself plenty of room to chip the ball and run it up close to the pin. Pars are scarce when you're chipping with little room between you and the pin.

425
IF THE GREEN SLOPES FROM BACK TO FRONT...
Err on missing short over missing long.
Downhill chips are more difficult to control than uphill chips. (Reverse this strategy if the green slopes from front to back.)

426
IF THERE IS TROUBLE FRONTING THE GREEN...
Hit the club that will easily carry the obstacle.
That's the club that will carry it even if you mis-hit the shot. You'd rather have a long putt or chip than a tricky explosion shot from the sand.

PLAY IT SMART ON THE TEE BOX
Tour-tested strategies for avoiding penalties and wasting shots

HOW TO ATTACK DOGLEGS ON WINDY DAYS
Play to your strengths, not your ego
By Mike Adams

You're on the tee of a 400-yard par 4 that doglegs to the left, and the pin is cut on the far left side of the green. There's tree trouble to the left of the fairway and water up the right side, and a stiff wind is blowing from left to right.

427
IF YOU CAN WORK THE BALL
Play a hold-up draw
Set up: Middle of tee box
Aim: Center of fairway
Swing: Play a draw with a 3-wood (it's easier to shape than a driver). The left-to-right wind and right-to-left shot shape should even out, putting you in the middle.
Pro: Takes water out of play.
Con: Overcook it and you'll be in the trees; undercook it and you're in the drink.

Always err on the opposite side of a dogleg. You can still make par even if you hit into the water.

428
IF YOU FEAR SHAPING SHOTS
Play into the wind
Set up: Toward right tee marker
Aim: Left side of fairway
Swing: Make your regular swing with either your driver or 3-wood and hit toward the left edge of the fairway. The wind should blow the ball back to the center.
Pro: No adjustments.
Con: Slight loss of distance.

Most of a hole's yardage occurs before the dogleg—hit only what you need to get past the bend and in the fairway.

429
IF YOU'RE A FADER
Ride the wind
Set up: Toward right marker
Aim: Up the left side
Swing: Hit your driver and start the ball up the edge of the treeline. The combined effects of the left-to-right wind and left-to-right spin should put you in the right side of the fairway.
Pro: Takes trees out of play
Con: None.

With the pin cut left, position A is the right side of the fairway because it gives you the clearest view of your target.

WIND DIRECTION

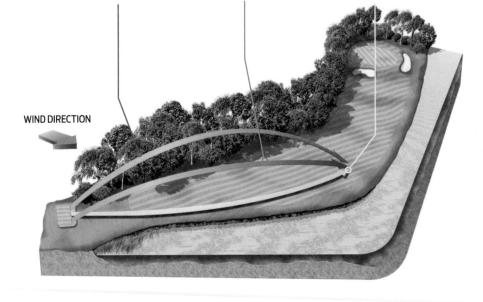

430

HOW TO SPOT TROUBLE
Look for miss spots and can't-miss spots to avoid all tee-shot trouble
By Brady Riggs

The key to hitting more greens is to plan your strategy from the tee box, not from your second shot. Here's how.

STEP 1
Stand on the tee and get a good sense of the hole. What you're looking for here are good miss spots.

STEP 2
If it's a dogleg left and there are trees on the left, move your target from the center of the fairway to the point between the center of the fairway and the right rough (opposite if the dogleg is reversed). If you miss left, you're still in the fairway and have a good shot into the green. If you miss right you're in the rough, but still have an open shot (what you wouldn't have if you aimed for the center of the fairway and missed left).

GOOD MISS

BAD MISS

Amateur

Pro

STEP 3
Don't assume you need an extra club or two to reach the green because your tee ball landed in the rough. For any club other than a wedge, you'll generate the same distance as if you were hitting from the fairway, but the ball will carry less and roll more.

SHAPE SHOTS AT WILL
Choose fade or draw by changing the way you step into the shot
By Jerry Mowlds

Stand with your feet together and the ball off the middle of your left foot.

431

TO DRAW IT
Step forward and out with your left foot. Notice how this move positions the ball back between the center of your chest and your right foot and tilts your spine to the right. With the ball teed here you're forced to make a more in-to-out downswing, which automatically puts right-to-left sidespin on the ball.

432

TO FADE IT
Step back and out with your right foot. This time, notice how the ball moves forward in your stance and points your shoulders left of the target. (You should feel your spine leaning slightly toward the target as well.) This position forces you to make a more descending, across-the-line blow and generate left-to-right spin.

SIX TOP 100 TEACHERS ON:

HITTING MORE GREENS FROM THE FAIRWAY

How to get it on and close from all lies and distances

433
Charlie King Says
EXPAND YOUR TARGET AREA

Pro landing area

Your landing area

434
Camilo Villegas says
FORGET ABOUT THE FLAGSTICK

435
Steve Bosdosh says
HOW TO HANDLE IN-BETWEEN DISTANCES

At the range, select a target you can easily reach with your 7-iron. Hit five balls at the target, and count how many land within a yard of it. If you land one ball or less within a yard, the flag is too narrow a target for you. Now stretch your target area to five yards on both sides of the flag and hit five more balls. **Keep stretching your target area five yards at a time until you can land three out of five balls in the target zone.** Take this target width to the course and lay it over the pin on every approach shot.

When I was younger I'd take dead aim at the flagstick on almost every approach—there were very few pins that I wouldn't go after, and I missed a lot of greens as a result. Now, I'm more apt to aim at the center of the green than directly at the pin, unless I'm playing catch-up and need to pull off a risky shot. If you're a mid-handicap golfer, it's a safe bet that **you'd save at least four strokes every round if you aimed for the middle of the green** on every approach.

You're in the fairway, but the yardage to the hole is five yards farther than what you can comfortably hit your 7-iron and five yards short of what you get with a good 6-iron swing. **If you're a 10 handicap or less** (or the pin is up and there's trouble long)...
...*hit the shorter club with a harder swing.*
If you're an 11 handicap or above (or the pin is back and there's trouble short)...
...*hit the longer club with a three-quarter swing.*

436

Dan Pasquariello says
SHAPE SHOTS WITH YOUR GRIP

FADE

DRAW

To hit it straight, reset your grip by turning your left wrist (not the club) until you can only see two knuckles on your left hand.

To hit an easy fade, set your left thumb at 12 o'clock on the grip and turn your left wrist (not the club) counterclockwise until you can only see one knuckle.

To hit an easy draw, set your left thumb at 1 o'clock and reset your grip by turning your left wrist (not the club) clockwise until you can see three knuckles.

437

Brady Riggs says
HIT DRIVER OFF THE DECK

Take a risk and try the most electrifying shot in golf: driver off the deck.
1: Aim your body to the left of your target to accommodate a fade ball flight and play the ball off your left heel.
2: Turn your shoulders under your head on your downswing so the club can swing to the left after impact.
3: At impact give the ball a karate chop with your left hand. This will help you keep your hands from over-rotating
4: Strive to hit the ball first and the turf second.

438

David Glenz on
HOW TO HANDLE ELEVATION RISES

Look at the flagstick and calculate how many of them you'd have to set below each other until the bottom of the last one was even with your ball. Take this number and multiply it by eight (the height of a flagstick in feet), and take that total and divide it by three to give you a number in yards. Subtract that number from the listed yardage to a green that's below you (or add it to the listed yardage to a green that's above you) to discover the true distance. Make your club selection based on that yardage.

MORE SMART PLAYS FROM THE FAIRWAY

Save strokes with these classic strategic plays on windy days and when playing long par 5s

439

KNOCK IT LOW INTO THE WIND

This boring bullet works in even the stiffest winds

By Ted Sheftic

You're in the fairway, mid-iron distance to the pin, with a stiff breeze in your face. You might think about making your normal swing with an extra club or two, but even the normal loft of a 5-iron could balloon into the wind and cause the ball to land way short of your target.

Better players use the knockdown shot in this situation. The controlled half-swing you'll make produces a low ball that stays below the wind and travels straight at the target. Take two extra clubs (a 6-iron, for example, if you're at your 8-iron distance) and follow the steps below.

ADDRESS
● Play the ball back in your stance—directly off the toes of your right foot.
● Forward press your hands so that the shaft leans toward the target.
● If your normal grip pressure is a "7" on a 1-to-10 scale, make it a "9" here.

BACKSWING
● Make a shorter, more compact backswing (notice that this doesn't mean restricting your shoulder and hip turn).
● Feel like your left arm is connected to your chest as you take the club back and swing it to the top.

DOWNSWING
● Concentrate on making an aggressive move from the top of your backswing.
● Try to keep your left arm firm. Use your body to move your straight left arm from a horizontal position to a vertical position at impact. Don't go soft on this shot!

FINISH
● Just like you did with your backswing, abbreviate your finish, but make sure that your head, chest, hips and knees are facing the target.
● The ball will come out low and hot—it will rise a little but settle quickly once it hits the turf.

HOW TO LAY UP SMART
You're not always going to be able to go for it. Here's how to play short of the green for birdie, not bogey
By Fred Griffin

Y ou're playing a long par 5, and while your drive is sitting in the fairway, the green is just too far away to think about going for it in two. The smart play is to hit a layup short of the green. If you're like most golfers, you almost always choose the same strategy: blasting your 3-wood as far as you can. This is the reason you often walk away from a par 5 with a nasty "7" on your scorecard. Before you attempt the longest possible shot (which is the easiest to hit off line, i.e. into the rough or other trouble), consider the three questions posed here.

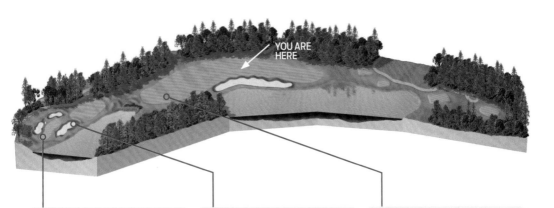

YOU ARE HERE

440
IS THE PIN CLEAR?
If the pin is in a favorable center position with no trouble in front, go ahead and blast away with your 3-wood. Pick a precise landing spot and make a smooth, controlled swing—don't try to "kill it." You'll have an unobstructed chip to the hole.

441
IS THE PIN PROTECTED?
With the pin behind a bunker on a firm green, being 20 to 30 yards away is not a good spot. You're not far away enough to put enough backspin on the ball to stop it, so even if you pure your second shot with a 3-wood, you're out of position. Select the club that will leave you with a full pitching wedge into the green.

442
WHAT'S YOUR FAVORITE CLUB?
If your distance control on full-wedge shots is inconsistent, but you always hit your 8-iron 140 yards, then pick a layup spot 140 yards from the green. Focus on that landing area as though it were the actual green. Laying up is a numbers game, and you want to hit yours on the money.

LEAVE YOURSELF EASIER PUTTS
Sometimes the best place to land your ball is away from the flagstick

THREE WAYS TO BEAT PAR 3s
Use your head to get the best of the short holes
By Shawn Humphries

Most of the damage a typical golfer inflicts on his card comes on par 3s. This might seem surprising, since these short holes can look pretty easy, but trouble usually lurks everywhere. If you want to lower your scores, you need to use your head before you make a swing.

443

CHOOSE WISELY
More than 90% of tee shots on par-3 holes come up short, leaving a tricky up and down. To make sure this doesn't happen to you, always pull the club that will get you to the back of the green on a solid strike.

446

THE STRATEGIC WAY TO MAKE MORE PUTTS
Some putts are just plain harder than others
By Brady Riggs

W hen you're planning your approach to the green or your recovery shot from the greenside rough or a bunker, don't always go for the close leave. The best play is to leave the ball on the correct section of the green. Consider the following:

Uphill putts are easier than downhill putts (so it's a good idea to leave your approach shots below the hole).

Right-to-left putts are easier than straight ones, and both of those are easier than a left-to-right putt (so it's a good idea to leave your shots on the right side of the pin if the green slopes from back to front and the left side of the pin if the green slopes from front to back).

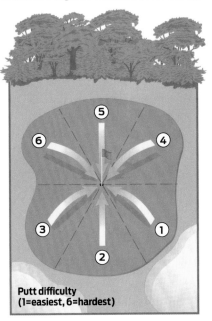

Putt difficulty (1=easiest, 6=hardest)

Straight putts have to be hit perfectly to go in. On right-to-left putts, you can play too much break and still find the bottom of the cup if you hit the putt soft (and play too little break and drain it if you hit the putt hard).

The worst combination is downhill and left-to-right— human beings don't make those.

444

GAUGE ELEVATION
Par 3s are tricky because they're rarely flat. There's usually some elevation change that tricks your eye and throws off your ability to gauge distance. Make sure you take elevation into account as well as the overall yardage before you select a club.

445

AIM CONSERVATIVELY
Since distance isn't a factor, most par 3s defend themselves at the green, usually in the form of bunkers and other hazards. It's funny—designers never place these defenses in the center of the green, but most golfers never aim there, either. Forget the pin and aim for the fat of the green. It's a recipe for consistent scoring.

IMPROVE EVERY TIME YOU PLAY
Use your rounds as practice guides to see which areas need the most work

447

RATE YOUR ROUND
A new tracking system tells you instantly where your scoring went awry
By Jerry Mowlds

The next time you play, keep a second scorecard. Label each row with "Putts, Shot 1, Shot 2, Shot 3, Shot 4," etc. Mark the score box for each shot to indicate the club used, whether or not you hit the fairway or green (X for hit, O for miss), the direction of your misses (with an arrow) and the quality of your contact ("3" for excellent contact, "2" for okay contact and "1" for poor contact). When you get to the green, write down the number of putts and the distance of your first and any remaining putts (see the card at right).

There are numerous score- and stat-tracking programs you can use to evaluate your game, but very few of them give you an indication of the quality of your ballstriking like this simple method. (You can still hit the fairway with a drop-kick skull off the tee). Plus, this tracking system provides you with instant feedback on the round you just played and holds the clues as to why you posted the score you wrote on your other card.

QUALITY METER
Scan the contact ratings of your first and second shots. If you see mostly 1s and 2s, you know that the quality of your strikes kept you from playing your best. Focus on improving contact during your next practice session.

ACCURACY METER
Scan the fairways- and greens-hit markings. If you see that you hit a lot of accurate shots but posted a higher-than-normal score, look to your putting stats. If you see mostly Os and not Xs, then you know your troubles came from hitting inaccurate drives and approaches.

HOW TO FILL OUT YOUR CARD
Fairway/green hit: **x**
Fairway/green missed: **o**
Excellent contact: **3**
Okay contact: **2**
Poor contact: **1**
First-putt distance/second-putt distance: **24/12**
Clubs: **3w, 5w, 3h, 3i, 4i...**

GHOST CREEK

1	328	372	392
	325	364	391
2		128	158
3	108		
	414	495	515
4	179	193	205
5		341	36
6	316		40
7	301	384	
8	462	497	
9	368	419	
Out	2801	3193	
10	410	453	
11	122	145	
12	327	37	
13	295	3	
14	167		
15	421		
16	97		

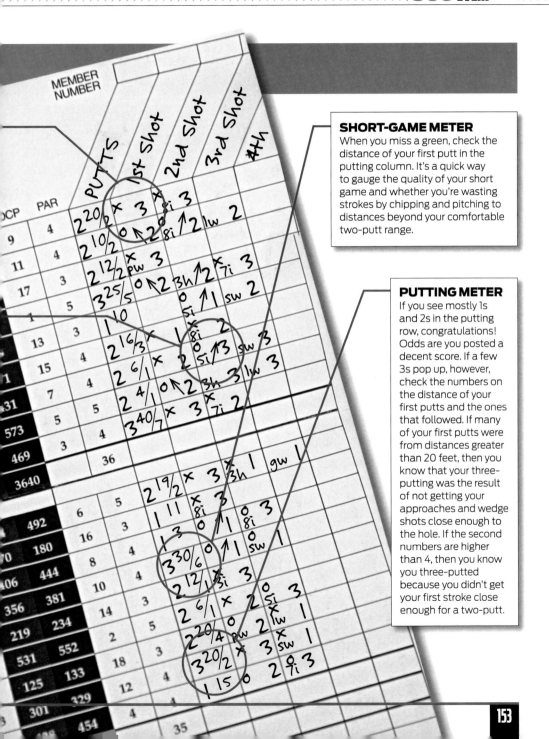

SHORT-GAME METER

When you miss a green, check the distance of your first putt in the putting column. It's a quick way to gauge the quality of your short game and whether you're wasting strokes by chipping and pitching to distances beyond your comfortable two-putt range.

PUTTING METER

If you see mostly 1s and 2s in the putting row, congratulations! Odds are you posted a decent score. If a few 3s pop up, however, check the numbers on the distance of your first putts and the ones that followed. If many of your first putts were from distances greater than 20 feet, then you know that your three-putting was the result of not getting your approaches and wedge shots close enough to the hole. If the second numbers are higher than 4, then you know you three-putted because you didn't get your first stroke close enough for a two-putt.

FAULT FIXES

How to repair your swing when it goes haywire—and keep your worst shots at bay—with 53 quick fixes from the pros who know best: the Top 100 Teachers in America.

448

BE YOUR OWN SWING DOCTOR

Use your reflection to diagnose and fix your own flaws
By Mike LaBauve

Let's assume that your address position is solid, with your back straight, knees flexed and your arms hanging underneath your shoulders. Find a full-length mirror and take your address position in front of it. Study your reflection and note the angle of your clubshaft. Have a friend place tape on the mirror along this line (we'll call this Line 1), and then another in the opposite direction (Line 2), so that the two lines intersect at 90 degrees. These lines hold the key to grooving an on-plane swing because they help you get your body and club in the correct positions on both the backswing and the follow-through.

449

THE ADDRESS CHECK

At setup, make sure your shaft mimics Line 1. Your forward bend toward the ball should position your back and head along Line 2. Now you're solid.

450

THE BACKSWING CHECK

Take your club back to just above waist height and stop. Look at the mirror and make sure your back and head still lie on Line 2 and that your shoulder turn and wrist hinge have placed the clubshaft along Line 1.

If you're not on the correct backswing plane, it's because you lifted the club with your hands more than you turned your upper body (shaft above Line 1). Or you whipped the club too far to the inside by turning your shoulders too level and not raising the club at all (shaft below Line 1). To get your club correctly on plane, all you need to do is turn your left shoulder under your chin and gently cock your wrists a full 90 degrees.

451

THE FOLLOW-THROUGH CHECK

Swing through impact and once again stop when your hands reach just above waist height. Again, study your reflection. Make sure that your clubshaft again rests on Line 1 and your head and back haven't strayed from Line 2.

The common error here is a clubshaft that lies above Line 1, because most golfers don't swing enough to the left, or if they do they don't execute enough hip turn. You really need both: an aggressive and full hip rotation, along with hand movement that brings your club across your chest (not away from it). Although most swings finish with the shaft over the left shoulder (above Line 1), the shaft goes left after impact before it travels up.

RANGE-TIME IMPROVEMENT
Consult these lessons first when hammering out the kinks on the practice tee

452

HOW TO ERASE A BAD BALL-STRIKING DAY

Tweak your setup to get the results you expect when you make your best swings
By Scott Sackett

You can chalk up just about any bad scoring day to bad alignment. When your swing feels solid, but the ball doesn't behave, you can bet that you're setting up for failure. Hit the practice range, pick out a target and lay two clubs on the ground about two feet apart and parallel to each other so that the lane between them points at your target. Run a third club from the inside shaft through your stance, forming a capital T. Next, place a ball against the inside shaft opposite the grip end of the third, and three consecutive balls to the left of the first so that they sit edge to edge.

453

IMPROVE STANCE WIDTH

Set both feet the same distance from the shaft that's lying perpendicular to your aim clubs. When adjusting stance width, make sure the shaft on the ground stays in line with your zipper.

454

TO IMPROVE CLUBFACE AIM

Point the center of your clubface down the lane created by the two shafts (i.e., at the target). The face will probably look closed to you, but it's not.

455

TO IMPROVE BODY AIM

Position your feet so that your toes point straight toward the inside shaft. Use the outside shaft to check that your shoulders are parallel to your toe line. Now you're correctly aligned parallel left of your target.

456

TO IMPROVE BALL POSITION

Place your practice ball opposite one of the four station balls. Use the right-most practice ball for wedge shots. Move to the next ball for your short irons, then the next for your long irons and woods. When teeing your driver, position your practice ball off the left-most station ball.

457

HOW TO PRACTICE LIKE A TOUR PLAYER
Improve your rhythm—and look cool doing it!
By John Elliott, Jr.

Watch Tour players on the driving range. Most pros follow a six-step procedure that takes them from ball to ball in a deliberate, measured way that mimics how they approach each shot on the golf course. If you copy that procedure, you're guaranteed to become a better ballstriker.

1: START HERE
Tip over a bucket of balls and, with your club in your right hand, pull a ball out of the pile and drag it over to a spot where you can hit it.

2: Stand behind your ball and pick your target. Step into address—first with your right foot and then with your left— while glancing at your target.

6: Now "present" the handle of the club to your right hand, release your left hand, and go back to Step 1. Now you're practicing like a pro!

5: As the ball comes to a stop, remove your right hand from the grip and allow the club to slide down the fingers of your left hand until it feels light and balanced in your hand.

4: Make a complete, balanced swing so that you're facing the target and most of your weight is on your left foot. Study the flight of your ball, and stay in this position until it has landed.

3: Once you're comfortable in your address position and have visualized your target line, waggle the club once or twice to loosen your wrists, and then swing away.

SIX TOP 100 TEACHERS ON:

HOW TO FIX A SLICE
Over 70 percent of weekend players slice. Here's how to make sure you're not among them.

458

Dr. Jim Suttie says
**DON'T SPIN
THE CLUBFACE**

You need to eliminate excessive forearm rotation in your backswing.
Step 1: Secure a tee under the Velcro flap of your glove so the pointed end points straight up.
Step 2: Make your backswing and stop when your hands are at waist height. If the tee is pointing at the sky, you've rotated your forearms too much and fanned the face open.
Step 3: Go back to address and take the club away again, this time being sure to keep the tee (and the back of your hand) pointing at the ball.

459

Mike Lopuszynski says
**START WITH A
CLOSED SETUP**

Take your normal address position, then lift your hands up to waist level so that the shaft of the club is parallel to the ground. Open your hands and rotate the grip of the club in a counterclockwise direction. **The toe of the club should be pointing slightly to your left**, to the 11 o'clock position. Now close your hands on the grip and lower the clubhead down. The look of a slightly closed clubface will be unusual at first, but just go ahead and make your swing. You should quickly feel—and see—a difference in your shots.

460

Kellie Stenzel says
**PIN YOUR LEFT ARM
TO YOUR CHEST**

You're setting up a slice by opening your clubface at the start of your backswing. You know you're guilty of this if you feel your left bicep move away from your chest as you start the club back. The solution is simple: **Keep the connection between your left bicep and your chest intact** as you swing your arms to start your backswing. Maintaining this connection stops your forearms from over-rotating in your backswing.

461
Anne Cain says
DON'T LET YOUR ELBOWS FLY

462
Dave Phillips says
THROW A PERFECT STRIKE!

463
Bryan Gathright says
GIVE YOUR SWING THE ELBOW

NO!

You tend to lift your right elbow to bring the club back as far as it can go in your backswing. This causes your arms to swing way past the point when they should naturally stop. Now you're headed for inconsistent contact and misses that go way high and to the right. Practice your backswing with a Nerf football wedged between your elbows. **Try to keep the ball from falling out by keeping your elbows together.** Make sure you complete your backswing with a full wrist cock.

Grab a baseball and give it a good hurl. As you do, **notice how you instinctively step forward with your front leg while simultaneously rearing back with your throwing arm.** That's the chain of events you need to build in your backswing to stop swinging over the top and hitting a slice. Your downswing isn't a unified motion. Move your lower body first and then your upper body, with your arms and clubhead bringing up the rear.

As you swing through impact, rotate your left elbow so that it points down at the ground [*main photo, above*]. This kind of elbow rotation allows your right hand to properly turn past your left—the real way to beat a tendency to slice. When you do it correctly, you'll **feel like your left elbow is actually bending instead of snapping straight.** When your left elbow stays soft, your right arm extends as if by magic. It's this right arm extension that gives your swing power and extra accuracy.

FOUR ERRORS, FOUR FIXES
Eliminate common mistakes by listening to your body

HIT EVERY SHOT BETTER
Stop copying the pros and build a swing that your body can actually handle
By Jon Tattersall

The following simple tests will show you how to hit the ball the way you want to without the complications that result from trying to mimic Tiger, Ernie and Phil. You'll be pleasantly surprised at how these shortcuts will improve the overall quality and consistency of your shots.

464 FAULT: TOO-LONG BACKSWING

Fix: Stand at attention and raise your right arm directly out at your side and bend your elbow at a 90-degree angle. From this position, try to bend your right forearm back as far as you can without moving the rest of your arm. This test measures your right-shoulder flexibility, which determines how far back you can swing your club.

Application: If your right forearm is in the fail zone *[red area]*, you have limited flexibility in your right shoulder. Stop your backswing when your hands reach this point *[photo, right]*.

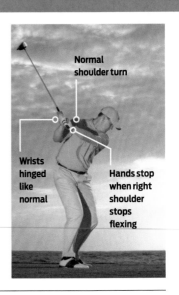

Normal shoulder turn

Wrists hinged like normal

Hands stop when right shoulder stops flexing

465 FAULT: POOR HIP TURN

Fix: Sit in a chair that allows you to rest both feet on the ground with a comfortable bend at both knees. Raise your right foot slightly off the ground and then try to move it laterally outward without moving your knee or upper leg. This test gauges your right-hip flexibility, which determines your ability to to increase the stretch between your upper and lower body and create coil.

Application: If your right leg is in the red fail zone at left , then your hip flexibility isn't up to snuff. Turn your hips *[photo, right]*. This allows you to make a full shoulder turn and load up powerfully behind the ball.

90-degree shoulder turn

Belt buckle pointing away from the target

Back facing the target

Braced right leg

Left knee behind the ball

466 FAULT: POOR POSTURE

Fix: Take the glute-muscle strength test. Lie down on your back and then pull your left foot toward your rear end as shown below. Lift your right leg and your rear end off the ground and hold for a count of 10. This test gauges the strength of your glutes (the muscles in your rear end). You need these to stay in your posture on your downswing and keep your spine angle intact through impact.

Application: If your right hip sags in the test, your glutes are weak and you have no chance of properly maintaining your spine angle. Make practice swings with a split grip [photo, right]. Focus on pulling the club into impact with your left hand and rotating the face to square with your right hand. This arms-dominated swing generates less force, which in turn makes it easier for you to maintain your posture when you swing.

467 FAULT: POOR RELEASE

Fix: Repeat the flexibility test in tip 464 but this time with your left arm. This test measures the flexibility of your left shoulder. The more flexible it is, the more you can swing your arms to the left after impact and release the club with your hands.

Application: If your left forearm is in the red fail zone pictured at left, then you have limited flexibility in your left shoulder. So instead of trying to rotate your forearms and wrists to release the club, keep your hands facing each other and continue to rotate your upper body toward the target until well after impact. In fact, you should feel like you're hitting the ball with your chest and that your hands are just along for the ride.

ULTIMATE PUTTING FIXES
Make your stroke extra-smooth and razor sharp with the help of a friend

HOW TO STOP YIPPING
Allow the ball to simply "get in the way"
By PGA Tour coach Marius Filmalter

Most yippers think of the ball as an impediment or as something they have to move. In fact, golfers only yip when there's a ball on the ground.

Try this drill and prove it to yourself. Set up to putt and have a friend place his finger on top of the ball. Your friend's job is two-fold: to keep the ball where it is on some strokes, and on others, to pull it back just before impact. His goal is to basically surprise you. What happens after a while is that you'll get

frustrated ("Is he going to move that damn ball or isn't he?"). Eventually you'll stop caring ("I don't give a damn what he does, I'm just going to make my stroke."). That's the breakthrough you're looking for. At that point, you'll find that you're actually making nice, yip-less putting strokes.

468

Ask a friend to either randomly pull the ball back just before impact, or to leave it.

469

By moving the ball or keeping it in place, your friend is helping you to lose your anticipation of impact.

470

Not knowing whether the ball will be there at impact or not teaches you to forget the ball and simply make your stroke.

HOW TO STOP FREEZING
Stalling at address leads to accuracy and distance-control problems

For this one you'll need your trusty friend again. Set up to putt with your friend next to you. The trick here is that you can't start your stroke until your friend taps you on the shoulder. You must wait for the command, which is exactly what you're missing

if you're a freezer. I know what you're saying—"I can't do this on the course." You can, in a way. Many of my students ring me after a round and tell me, "I know you weren't playing with us today, but I could feel your tap on my shoulder."

471 Set up to putt, but don't pull the trigger until your friend taps you on the shoulder.

472 The tap gives you a physical cue to replace the mental one you're missing.

473 The tap on your shoulder is the password to initiate the program in your brain that controls your stroke. You now have a physical command to replace the mental one that's missing.

SIX TOP 100 TEACHERS ON:

PRACTICE DRILLS THAT FIX EVERY FAULT

Try these range-only regimens to make your swing shine almost overnight

---

474

Dr. Jim Suttie says

TURN AWAY YOUR HOOK OR SLICE

L ay an iron on the ground next to your right foot as shown. Hold your driver across your chest at your shoulder line and make your backswing turn. Use the club on the ground as a guide: When you finish your turn your driver should point somewhere between the ball and the club on the ground. The only way to achieve this position is to turn your shoulders at a right angle to your spine and keep your head still. Since your spine is titled forward, **it should feel like your left shoulder is turning under your chin.**

475

Donald Crawley says

SYNC UP TO STOP THREE ERRORS

Backswing

Downswing

A ddress a ball with any club, but place your right hand under your left armpit as shown. Swing your left arm back. With your right hand off the club **it should be easy to hinge the club up**, eliminating a late wrist cock. Next, pull back with your right arm and get your torso behind the ball. Notice how your weight moves onto your right leg, and your reverse pivot disappears. Swing back down by holding your left side in place as you drop your arms and club and start to unwind your hips. *Au revoir,* cut-swing path.

476

Brian Mogg says

GROOVE AN IN-OUT POWER PATH

T ee up a ball and place a second tee six inches and 45 degrees outside the first as shown. Try to sweep the ball off the first tee and swing over the second tee as you sling your clubhead through the hitting area. **This simulates the feel of proper extension through impact,** and swinging from inside the target line to the outside. You'll struggle to make good contact at first, but after a few attempts you'll start to see straighter shots, and even a few that draw powerfully from right to left.

477

John Elliott, Jr. says

SWING CROSS-HANDED FOR A PURER RELEASE

Swing a 7-iron with a cross-handed grip and you'll ingrain three keys that are difficult to perfect using a normal grip.

Needed hinge: Since your right hand is on top, your right wrist will hinge sooner and establish an extra lever for power.

Proper arm positioning: The cross-handed grip forces your right arm to fold correctly as your left arm remains straight.

The power approach: You'll also feel a bent right elbow and extended left arm deep into your downswing—vital for power.

478

Mike Lopuszynski says

FINE-TUNE YOUR DRIVING AIM

Stick two umbrellas (or dowels, or broken shafts) into the ground a few feet in front of you and hit balls through them without any thought of the landing area. Hitting through a gate like this gives you extra leeway to start your ball on the target line, and **this freedom will show up in your swing.** When you become too target-oriented you'll worry more about missing and end up making a rigid, overly careful swing. On the course, picture the umbrellas in your mind's eye and make the same smooth swing.

479

Bruce Patterson says

DROP YOUR FOOT BACK FOR A POWER PATH

If you can't seem to start the ball online or finish in the fairway, try this tip. Take a very narrow stance, then drop your front foot back about a foot. Tee up the ball and try to hit shots without losing your balance. **This drill forces you to swing your arms more in front of your body** and keeps the path from being too shallow and too in-to-out. Expect fewer pop-ups and slices and a lot more boring, fairway-finding drives.

FAST FIXES FOR BIG MISTAKES
You won't reach your potential until you've eliminated the game's most damaging mistakes

480
STOP YOUR CHICKEN WING
Eliminate slicing and weak hits using your own shirt
By Dr. Jim Suttie

If you slice, then there's a good chance that your left arm is breaking down through impact, with your elbow bent and pointing toward the target—the dreaded "chicken wing."

My simple fix is this: Tuck the sleeve of your shirt under your left arm at address. Then, make some slow-motion swings while keeping the sleeve of your shirt tucked under your arm—it should feel like you're trapping the sleeve between your arm and body.

NO!

YES!

481
STOP WRIST BREAKDOWN
Curing this ailment sets your clubface perfectly square for massive hits
By Shawn Humphries

Make practice backswings with your wristwatch on your left wrist. Before you start, slide a pen under the face so that the cap end reaches the middle of the back of your left hand as shown. As you swing to the top, can you feel the cap dig into the back of your left hand? If so, you're cupping your left wrist. A cupped left wrist causes your clubface to rotate wide open at the top. Unless you make a serious compensating move, the face will stay open on your downswing. Continue to practice your backswing with the pen under your watch until you can bring the club to the top without the pen jamming into your hand. Keep your left wrist perfectly flat.

482

STOP SWINGING OVER THE TOP
Fix this slice-causer with your hip turn
By Steve Bosdosh

Set up to a ball and imagine a friend behind you grabbing your right pocket. When you're ready to swing, feel your "friend" yank your right hip away from the ball and behind you. Although it's not really happening, this kind of hip action puts you in a position that makes it difficult to swing over the top. As you start down, feel a tug again, but this time on your left hip. This will help you approach the ball from the inside—from the lower right corner of your vision—and hit a draw.

483

STOP REVERSE PIVOTING
Use your bag to set your weight where it should be
By Peter Krause

With your bag around your shoulders, set up in your normal address position with an iron and make a half-speed swing. If you sway to the left at the top or hang back on your right side in your follow-through, the bag will immediately let you know: the bottom of the bag will sag toward the ground if you do the former, and the top end will do the same if you're guilty of the latter (probably dumping your clubs in the process). Continue to swing until the bag remains in place against the small of your back.

484

STOP STEERING THE BALL
A proper release elevates the quality of your strikes in a heartbeat
By Mike Malaska

Swing an iron slowly to the top of your backswing. Make an equally slow downswing and stop when the shaft is parallel to the ground. If your left elbow is pointing directly at the target, you've found the reason why you hit pushes and slices. Your left elbow should be pointing left of the target, not at it, when the shaft is parallel with the ground. This means you're properly rotating the clubface so that it will be square when it contacts the ball.

NO!

YES!

SIX TOP 100 TEACHERS ON:

FIXING EVERY BAD BALL FLIGHT
How to instantly nix the poor strikes that have been ruining your scores

485	486	487

Jim Hardy on
HOW TO STOP A SNAP HOOK

Dr. Gary Wiren on
HOW TO STOP BLADING SHOTS

Jim Murphy on
HOW TO STOP FAT CONTACT

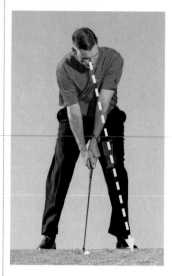

You snap it when your right hand slips underneath your left in the downswing. The clubface swings open, and the only way to get it square is to arch your right wrist and snap the clubface—and the ball—to the left. To fix it, **keep the heel of your right palm on the grip on the way back down** so it doesn't slip and force you to make the snap compensation. Take a tee and place it between your two hands as you grip the club. Hit balls on the range and make sure that the tee doesn't come out during your swing.

One of the reasons you're blading the ball is because you're moving your swing center past the ball in your downswing. Here's a new use for a training-aid stalwart—the Impact Bag—that's sure to fix your sliding problems. Instead of placing the bag where the ball is when you practice your impact position, wedge it between your ankles. As you make the transition from backswing to downswing, **squeeze the Impact Bag between your ankles firmly.** This should make it impossible to slide forward.

The solution for fat contact is to make a steeper downswing. The trick is to move the bottom of your swing arc forward so it matches where the ball sits in your stance. The easiest way to accomplish this is to turn your head to the left and **focus your eyes on a spot two feet in front of the ball** (toward the target). Your instinct favors striking where your eyes point, and if they point ahead of the ball the bottom of your swing arc will automatically move forward. You'll catch the ball first, then the turf.

488

Peter Krause on
**HOW TO STOP
WEAK IMPACT**

If you're prone to hitting weak shots with your irons, then you're probably hanging too far back and pivoting around your right leg through impact (instead of your left). This causes you to release the club early and swing with a lifting or scooping motion. Start your downswing with your left knee and hip **"posting up" on top of your left foot first.** As your left hip begins to clear out of the way, your right knee and hip move up into the ball, allowing you to deliver the club into the ball with power and accuracy.

489

Shawn Humphries on
**HOW TO STOP
TOE HITS**

You're too steep and cutting across the ball. An easy way to remedy the problem is to think about **keeping your elbows level at the top.** Take the club back and find your position at the top. Then, have a friend grab another club from your bag—something long like your driver or 3-wood—and try to balance it between your arms. If your elbows aren't level, the club won't be straight. Practice this until you can feel the correct position all the time.

490

Tim Mahoney on
**HOW TO STOP
THIN CONTACT**

It's important that you create a balanced stance over the ball at address and maintain that balance throughout your swing. This involves **keeping your head still and turning to the top while keeping your weight evenly distributed over both feet.** Try this: Turn your back to the sun so that you cast a shadow over the ball. Settle into your stance with the ball positioned in the middle of the shadow created by your head. As you make your backswing, look at your shadow and check that it covers the ball as you swing.

SHORT-GAME FIXES
Restore confidence in your wedge play with these proven tips and drills

491
HOW TO STOP BLADING CHIPS
Stand taller to avoid the grass behind the ball
By Tim Mahoney

Stop bending over so much! When you hunch over the ball excessively (a common error on delicate short shots) you're bound to rise up in reaction. Stand tall to the ball with long arms. Moreover, allow your arms to lengthen on your downswing and try to brush the grass in front of the ball.

NO! YES!

DRILL: REACH OUT
Address the ball in a taller posture and align the leading edge of your club just below the equator of the ball. Stay loose on your forward stroke and allow your arms to lengthen. If you do, your club will bottom out in front of the ball like it should. "Under-reaching" at address gives you a better margin for error to create crisp contact.

492
HOW TO STOP SHANKING
Change your takeaway to avoid this short-shot disaster
By Tim Mahoney

You shank when you flip the clubhead behind your hands on your takeaway. This moves the impact point from the clubface to the hosel. To make sure that you don't do it again, imagine that the clubface is a mirror. At any point during the stroke, your ball should be able to look back and see its reflection.

NO!

YES!

DRILL: WHIP STOP
Practice chipping while holding the club with your thumbs and forefingers only *[below]*. It's an odd hold that teaches you to maintain a light grip pressure. That's all you need to control the club and make sure it doesn't get behind your hands.

493

HOW TO STOP FLUBBING SHORT SHOTS

Keep your hands ahead of the clubface and never come up short again

By Chuck Winstead

When you take your normal chipping stance with your feet close together and the ball played just back of center, notice how your shaft leans toward the target, forming a lower-case "y" with your forearms. Make sure the "y" exists in your address position, but don't think about keeping it intact at impact. Your goal is to make your impact position as smooth and natural as possible, without having to think about it. Instead, make sure the "y" is intact when you swing the club back and that it's still there when you finish your swing. If you can manage to make a "y" between your forearms and clubshaft before and after impact, you'll guarantee that it will be there when you strike the ball.

494

HOW TO STOP YANKING CHIPS LEFT

To hold the line, let the clubface square itself

By Rick McCord

If you consciously make an effort to square the clubface at impact, you probably do so too soon, and that closes the face and sends the ball left of your target. What you should do is concentrate on bringing the club into impact from the inside—in other words, try to make contact halfway between the back of the ball and the side of the ball facing your feet. Set some tees on the ground to guide you on the correct path. The club will continue to close as it moves through impact, but it will be closing to a square position, rather than to a position that will send the ball dead left.

Just like you should in your full swing, attack the ball from the inside on all chips.

SAVE FOUR SHOTS BY SATURDAY
Eliminating the following errors from your game will keep big numbers off your scorecard

SHOT 1:
HIGH, WEAK SHORT IRON
Never miss the green from short range again
By Tim Mahoney

You're scooping the ball in an attempt to hit the shot high. Scooping leans the shaft away from the target at impact and invariably opens the face, hence the short and right miss.

495
BACKSWING
As you reach the top of your backswing, think about moving the clubhead from its high position to a low position in front of the ball.

496
IMPACT
Keep your hands ahead of the clubhead on your downswing and, more important, at impact. Your goal is to make a divot in front of the ball, not behind it or under it.

497
RELEASE
Resist the urge to lift and scoop by keeping the clubhead low to the ground after impact. It should feel like the shaft is an extension of your right forearm.

A good way to see if you're doing it correctly is to position the shadow of your head over the ball at address. On your downswing, move your body slightly toward the target so that your head is ahead of the ball at impact (check your shadow as shown). This helps you hit the ball first and take a divot second.

498
SHOT 2: POPPED-UP DRIVE
How to hit it flush, not float it up
By Tim Mahoney

NO!

When you pop up a tee shot, you make the mistake of sliding your left shoulder—and the bottom of your swing arc—in front of the ball on your downswing, so the clubhead is still descending when it contacts the ball. Try to keep your left shoulder even with the back of the ball on your downswing. Also, tee the ball higher so that the bottom of the ball is even with the top of your clubhead, and set the ball two inches inside your left heel and tilt your spine to the right at address.

499
SHOT 3: PULLED SHORT PUTT
Try this grip-pressure check to see if your right hand is taking over
By Dr. T.J. Tomasi

PULLED

STRAIGHT

Most right-handed players grip the club tighter with their right hand than their left. This uneven grip pressure causes you to flip the putterhead past your hands through impact and pull the putt left. Wrap some aluminum foil around the grip of your putter, and then roll some Play-Doh over the foil, creating an impression pad. Roll a few putts, then check the indentations made on the handle. If you see deep imprints *[above, left]*, your grip is too tight, and you're probably flipping the putterhead past your hands. Lighten your grip until you can make your stroke without making deep imprints.

500
SHOT 4: SAND SHOT LEFT IN BUNKER
The goal is always the same: escape on your first swing
By Tim Mahoney

There's only one way to leave a shot in the bunker: take too much sand. If you take too much sand it's usually because you mistakenly use your normal wedge swing, which is very steep and up-and-down. Your swing for a standard bunker lie needs to be wider and flatter. Plop down a few balls in a practice bunker and get down on your knees. This isn't a trick shot, but a practice drill to get you in the habit of swinging on the correct plane. Choke down on the grip a few inches and make your best effort to get the ball out. With a shorter posture you're forced to swing around your body, not so up and down.

GOLF MAGAZINE
TOP 100 TEACHERS IN AMERICA

The Best Instructors in the Game

There are more than 28,000 PGA of America members, and *GOLF Magazine* uses only the 100 most elite among them to help you lower your scores, improve your swing, hammer the ball longer and putt the lights out.

Mike Adams
Hamilton Farm G.C.
Gladstone, N.J.
mikeadamsgolf.com

Rob Akins
Spring Creek Ranch
Collierville, Tenn.
robakinsgolf.com

Eric Alpenfels
Pinehurst Resort
Pinehurst, N.C.
pinehurst.com

Todd Anderson
Sea Island Golf
Learning Center
St. Simons Island, Ga.
seaisland.com

Robert Baker
Logical Golf
Miami Beach, Fla.
logicalgolf.com

Jimmy Ballard
Ballard Swing
Connection
Key Largo, Fla.
jimmyballardgolf.com

Mike Bender
Timacuan Golf Club
Lake Mary, Fla.
mikebender.com
*2009 PGA TEACHER
OF THE YEAR*

Steve Bosdosh
Members Club at
Four Streams
Beallsville, Md.
stevebosdoshgolf.com

Michael Breed
Sunningdale
Country Club
Scarsdale, N.Y.
www.michaelbreed.com

Brad Brewer
Brad Brewer Golf
Academy at Shingle
Creek Resort
Orlando, Fla.
bradbrewer.com

Henry Brunton
Henry Brunton
Golf Academy
Maple, Ontario, Canada
henrybrunton.com

Jason Carbone
Baltusrol Golf Club
Springfield, N.J.

Chuck Cook
Chuck Cook
Golf Academy
Austin, Tex.
chuckcookgolf.com
*1996 PGA TEACHER
OF THE YEAR*

Donald Crawley
Boulders Golf Academy
Carefree, Ariz.
golfsimplified.com

Mike Davis
Walters Golf Academy
Las Vegas, Nev.
waltersgolf.com

Glenn Deck
Pelican Hill Resort
Newport Coast, Calif.
pelicanhill.com

Dom DiJulia
Dom DiJulia
School of Golf
New Hope, Pa.
dijuliagolf.com

Krista Dunton
Berkeley Hall
Bluffton, S.C.
kristadunton.com
*2002 LPGA TEACHER
OF THE YEAR*

John Elliott, Jr.
Golden Ocala Golf and
Equestrian Club
Ocala, Fla.
jmegolf.com

Chuck Evans
Medicus Golf Schools
Destin, Fla.
*medicusgolfinstitute.
com*

Bill Forrest
Troon Country Club
Scottsdale, Ariz.
billforrestgolf.com
*2006 PGA TEACHER
OF THE YEAR*

Eden Foster
Maidstone Club
East Hampton, N.Y.

Bryan Gathright
Oak Hills Country Club
San Antonio, Tex.

David Glenz
David Glenz
Golf Academy
Franklin, N.J.
davidglenz.com
*1998 PGA TEACHER
OF THE YEAR*

Rick Grayson
Rivercat Golf Club
Springfield, Mo.
rickgraysongolf.com

Fred Griffin
Grand Cypress
Academy of Golf
Orlando, Fla.

Ron Gring
Gring Golf at Timber
Creek Golf Club
Daphne, Ala.
gringgolf.com

Lou Guzzi
Lou Guzzi Golf Academy
Talamore Country Club
Ambler, Pa.
louguzzi.com

Mark Hackett
Old Palm Golf Club
Palm Beach
Gardens, Fla.

Martin Hall
Ibis Golf & Country Club
West Palm Beach, Fla.
*2008 PGA TEACHER
OF THE YEAR*

Joseph Hallet
PGA Center for Learning
and Performance
Port St. Lucie, Fla.

Hank Haney
Hank Haney Golf
McKinney, Tex.
hankhaney.com
*1993 PGA TEACHER
OF THE YEAR*

Jim Hardy
Jim Hardy Golf
Houston, Tex.
jimhardygolf.com
*2007 PGA TEACHER
OF THE YEAR*

Craig Harmon
Oak Hill Country Club
Rochester, N.Y.

Butch Harmon, Jr.
Butch Harmon
School of Golf
Henderson, Nev.
butchharmon.com

Mike Hebron
Smithtown Landing G.C.
Smithtown, N.Y.
mikehebron.com
*1991 PGA TEACHER
OF THE YEAR*

Shawn Humphries
Cowboys Golf Club
Grapevine, Tex.
shawnhumphries.com

Ed Ibarguen
Duke University
Golf Club
Durham, N.C.
golf.duke.edu

Eric Johnson
Oakmont Country Club
Oakmont, Pa.

Hank Johnson
Greystone Golf Club
Birmingham, Ala.
*2004 PGA TEACHER
OF THE YEAR*

Charlie King
Reynolds Golf Academy
at Reynolds Plantation
Greensboro, Ga.
*reynoldsgolfacademy.
com*

Jerry King
Kapalua Golf Academy
Lahaina, Maui, Hi.
jerrykinggolf.com

Peter Kostis
Kostis/McCord
Learning Center
Scottsdale, Ariz.
*kostismccordlearning.
com*

Peter Krause
Hank Haney Int'l
Junior Golf Academy
Hilton Head, S.C.
peterkrausegolf.com

Mike LaBauve
Westin Kierland Resort
Scottsdale, Ariz.
kierlandresort.com

Rod Lidenberg
Prestwick Golf Club
Woodbury, Minn.
pgamasterpro.com

Jack Lumpkin
Sea Island Golf
Learning Center
St. Simons Island, Ga.
seaisland.com
*1995 PGA TEACHER
OF THE YEAR*

Keith Lyford
Golf Academy at
Old Greenwood
Truckee, Calif.
lyfordgolf.net

Tim Mahoney
Talking Stick
Golf Course
Scottsdale, Ariz.
timmahoneygolf.com

Mike Malaska
Superstition Mountain
Apache Junction, Ariz.
malaskagolf.com

Brian Manzella
English Turn Golf &
Country Club
New Orleans, La.
brianmanzella.com

Paul Marchand
Shadowhawk Golf Club
Richmond, Tex.

Lynn Marriott
Vision 54
Phoenix, Ariz.
vision54.com
*1992 LPGA TEACHER
OF THE YEAR*

Rick McCord
McCord Golf Academy
at Orange Lake C.C.
Orlando, Fla.
*themccordgolfacademy.
com*

Mike McGetrick
Colorado Golf Club
Parker, Colo.
coloradogolfclub.com
*1999 PGA TEACHER
OF THE YEAR*

Jim McLean
Jim McLean Golf School
Miami, Fla.
jimmclean.com
*1994 PGA TEACHER
OF THE YEAR*

Brian Mogg
Brian Mogg
Performance Center at
Golden Bear Golf Club
at Keene's Point
Windermere, Fla.
moggperformance.com

Bill Moretti
Moretti Golf
Austin, Tex.
morettigolf.com

Jerry Mowlds
Pumpkin Ridge
Golf Club
North Plains, Ore.

Scott Munroe
Adios Golf Club
Coconut Creek, Fla.
moneygolf.net

Jim Murphy
Jim Murphy Golf
at Sugar Creek C.C.
Sugar Land, Tex.
jimmurphygolf.com

Tom Ness
Reunion Golf Club
Hoschton, Ga.
affinitigolfacademy.com

Pia Nilsson
Vision 54
Phoenix, Ariz.
vision54.com

Dan Pasquariello
The Club at
St. James Plantation
Southport, N.C.

Tom Patri
Friar's Head Golf Club
Riverhead, N.Y.
tompatri.com

Bruce Patterson
Butler National
Golf Club
Oak Brook, Ill.

Dave Pelz
Dave Pelz Golf
Spicewood, Tex.
pelzgolf.com

Mike Perpich
RiverPines Golf
Alpharetta, Ga.
mikeperpich.com

Gale Peterson
Sea Island Golf
Learning Center
St. Simons Island, Ga.
seaisland.com

E.J. Pfister
Oak Tree National
Golf Club
Edmond, Okla.
ejpfistergolf.com

David Phillips
Titleist Performance
Institute
Oceanside, Calif.
mytpi.com

Carol Preisinger
The Kiawah Island Club
Kiawah Island, SC
carolpreisinger.com
*1998 LPGA TEACHER
OF THE YEAR*

Kip Puterbaugh
The Aviara
Golf Academy
Carlsbad, Calif.
aviaragolfacademy.com

Nancy Quarcelino
Kings Creek G.C.
Spring Hill, Tenn.
qsog.com
*2000 LPGA TEACHER
OF THE YEAR*

Carl Rabito
Bolingbrook G.C.
Bolingbrook, Ill.
rabitogolf.com

Dana Rader
Dana Rader Golf School
at Ballantyne Resort
Charlotte, N.C.
danarader.com
*1990 LPGA TEACHER
OF THE YEAR*

Brad Redding
The Resort Club at
Grande Dunes
Myrtle Beach, S.C.
grandedunes.com

Brady Riggs
Woodley Lakes
Golf Course
Van Nuys, Calif.
bradyriggs.com

Phil Ritson
Orange County
National Golf Center
Orlando, Fla.
ocngolf.com

Scott Sackett
Scott Sackett Golf
Scottsdale, Ariz.
scottsackett.com

Adam Schriber
Crystal Mountain Resort
Thompsonville, Mich.
crystalmountain.com

Craig Shankland
LPGA International
Daytona Beach, FL
*2001 PGA TEACHER
OF THE YEAR*

Mike Shannon
Sea Island Golf
Learning Center
St. Simons Island, Ga.
seaisland.com

Ted Sheftic
Bridges Golf Club
Abbottstown, Pa.
tedsheftic.com

Laird Small
Pebble Beach
Golf Academy
Pebble Beach, Calif.
*2003 PGA TEACHER
OF THE YEAR*

Randy Smith
Royal Oaks Country Club
Dallas, Tex.
*2002 PGA TEACHER
OF THE YEAR*

Rick Smith
Treetops Resort
Gaylord, Mich.
ricksmith.com

Todd Sones
Impact Golf Schools
at White Deer Run
Golf Club
Vernon Hills, Ill.
toddsones.com

Charles Sorrell
Crystal Lake
Country Club
Hampton, Ga.
sorrellgolf.com
*1990 PGA TEACHER
OF THE YEAR*

Mitchell Spearman
Doral Arrowwood
Golf Resort
Rye Brook, N.Y.
mitchellspearman.com

Mark Steinbauer
Carlton Woods
The Woodlands, Tex.
thewoodlands.com

Kellie Stenzel
Sebonack Golf Club
Southampton, N.Y.
kelliestenzelgolf.com

Tom Stickney
The Club at Cordillera
Vail, Colo.
tomstickneygolf.com

Dr. Jim Suttie
Cog Hill Golf Club
Lemont, Ill.
jimsuttie.com
*2000 PGA TEACHER
OF THE YEAR*

Jon Tattersall
Golf Performance
Partners
Terminus Club
Atlanta, Ga.
golfpp.com

Dr. T.J. Tomasi
Tomasi Golf
Port St. Lucie, Fla.
tjtomasi.com

J.D. Turner
The Turner Golf Group
Savannah, Ga.
jdturnergolf.com

Stan Utley
Grayhawk Learning Ctr.
Scottsdale, Ariz.
stanutleygolf.com

Chuck Winstead
The University Club
Baton Rouge, La.
universityclubbr.com

Dr. David Wright
Wright Balance Golf
Academy at Arroyo
Trabuco Golf Club
Mission Viejo, CA
wrightbalance.com

TOP 100 TEACHERS IN AMERICA HALL OF FAME

Peggy Kirk Bell
Pine Needles Resort
Southern Pines, N.C.
*pineneedles-
midpines.com*

Manuel De La Torre
Milwaukee Country Club
River Hills, Wisc.
*manueldelatorregolf.
com*
*1986 PGA TEACHER
OF THE YEAR*

Jim Flick
Taylor Made
Performance and
Research Lab
Carlsbad, Calif.
jimflick.com
*1988 PGA TEACHER
OF THE YEAR*

David Leadbetter
David Leadbetter
Golf Academy
Champions Gate, Fla.
davidleadbetter.com

Eddie Merrins
Bel-Air Country Club
Los Angeles, Calif.
eddiemerrins.com

Bob Toski
Toski-Battersby Golf
Learning Center
Coconut Creek, Fla.
learn-golf.com

Dr. Gary Wiren
Trump International
West Palm Beach, Fla.
garywiren.com
*1987 PGA TEACHER
OF THE YEAR*

TOP 100 TEACHERS IN AMERICA ADJUNCT

Mark Blackburn
The Ledges
Country Club
Huntsville, Ala.
blackburngolf.com

Bari Brandwynne
The Golf Academy L.A.
Los Angeles, Calif.
thegolfacademyla.com

John Callahan
John Callahan
Golf Center
Colchester, Conn.

Eric Eshleman
Country Club
of Birmingham
Birmingham, Ala.

Chris O'Connell
Plane Truth
Golf Institute
Spring, Tex.
planetruthgolf.com

Don Sargent
Scioto Country Club
Columbus, Ohio

Gary Weir
Westchester
Country Club
Rye, N.Y.